"Men can do it and we need to talk about that more.
A very timely book."

Fiona Millar,
author, The Secret World of the Working Mother

"Gideon Burrows perceptively and powerfully takes on the
last taboo in childcare, challenging the very foundations
of the contemporary debate about parenting."

Duncan Fisher OBE,
co-founder, The Fatherhood Institute and Dad.info

"An engaging manifesto: proof that dads can be capable
and caring when it comes to babies."

Oliver James,
broadcaster, child psychologist and parenting author

"Tackling a taboo subject is tricky, not to mention brave.
Burrows cleverly weaves humour, honest admissions and solid
research into this unavoidably contentious subject."

Junior magazine

An extended love letter to Sarah, Erin and Reid

Gideon Burrows is a writer, small business owner and involved father. He only realised other men didn't do an equal share of childcare when it was already too late to change. Just like his wife, he spends half the working week looking after their children. He lives close to the sea in Essex, owns five bicycles and grows 13 varieties of chillies.

www.mencandoit.co.uk

First published in Great Britain in 2013 by
ngo.media limited

Men Can Do It
The real reason dads don't do childcare and what
men and women should do about it

A catalogue record for this book is available
from the British Library.

Paperback ISBN: 978-0-9553695-3-7
Kindle ebook ISBN: 978-0-9553695-4-4
Other ebook ISBN: 978-0-9553695-5-1

Published by ngo.media limited
Austons, Layer Road, Abberton CO5 7NH
Company registration number: 04916846

2 4 6 8 10 9 7 5 3 1

Cover illustration: Martin Hargreaves

Design: Chandler Book Design,
www.chandlerbookdesign.co.uk

Printed and bound in Great Britain by
CPI Group (UK), Croydon,
CR0 4YY

Men Can Do It!

**The real reason dads don't do childcare
and what men and women should do about it**

GIDEON BURROWS

CONTENTS

INTRODUCTION

The Babysitter Bites Back

THERE'S A CLEVER little balancing technique that I call the toilet squat. Men who take their baby to the park or to the shops have to learn it for themselves very quickly. The trick is to change the baby's freshly filled nappy without anything – the change bag, the new nappy, the baby's freshly washed clothes, your hands or knees, and especially any part of your baby – touching the filthy, pissy men's toilet floor.

With change bag dangling precariously across the shoulder and baby wipes pre-prepared and sticking out of the top, you squat on tip-toes and sit on your heels. Baby is held on your knees with one arm under the armpits, with their legs jammed into your gut for stability, while the other hand switches alternately between grasping the sink for balance and, item by item, extracting baby from shoes, sodden babygrow and stinky nappy.

You then, still with the use of just one hand, dispose of same appropriately, wipe bottom thoroughly and deftly rebuild: new nappy, new babygrow, replace socks and booties, and all before your calves cramp up and down tumbles Daddy, baby and all.

The toilet squat works best when the child is in a docile mood, when Dad is relaxed and the damage done by the baby's bowels is not too severe. In fact, that's the only time it works.

Public toilets aren't built for men with babies. Any baby-change facility, if it exists at all, can be found in the women's loo or in a disabled toilet that seems to require a call to the Mayor themselves to get a key. The difficult choice for men is whether to dash into the ladies and lock the door (should a lock even exist) and risk being taken for some filthy lavatory loiterer. Or to squat.

It was after a somewhat challenging episode of this particular manoeuvre, this time in the back of an otherwise sweet little coffee shop in central London, that my thoughts on a book on the subject of equal parenting started to solidify. I was still in recovery from changing six-month-old Erin like this, balanced against the door in a cupboard-sized men's lav, when the 20-something waiter sauntered over to our table to offer me a refill.

"Ahhh," he cooed as she manically bashed the table with the pepper grinder. "You look like you've got your hands full. Are you babysitting today?"

That question.

In just six months of my child's life I'd already been asked it a dozen times. Nearly five years later, with my son Reid added to the mix, I've lost count of how many. The implication is clear. Mum is shopping (this was Covent Garden after all) or sharing a Jacob's Creek with girlfriends at All Bar One round the corner. I'm holding the fort, keeping the baby quiet by stuffing it with scone until she gets back.

I turned my head slowly upwards, fixed the waiter with a death stare I didn't realise I possessed, and snapped back:

"Is it even possible to babysit your own child?"

The poor lad just looked confused. He smiled thinly then retreated to another table to brighten up someone else's day. It wasn't his fault. He probably thought he was reaching out. But in my post-toilet squat mood all I could think of was: would you say the same thing to my wife?

There's a compelling and popular media image of new fatherhood. Men strolling comfortably and proudly around town, baby strapped cosily into their chest or nestled into a space-age travel system pushed expertly in front. These days men delightedly wipe gooey noses, merrily change nappies without blinking, and enthusiastically row, row, row the boat gently down the stream at playgroups the length and breadth of the UK.

Yet my presence with my own baby daughter in central London, having a cup of coffee, or going to the shops, or catching a bus, can still be deemed so unusual that it warrants puzzled comments: what could a man possibly be doing with a baby – on a weekday?

The new fatherhood story (which never included tales of men squatting on toilet floors anyway) turns out to be a fairytale. The picture is warm and cuddly, and makes us feel good about how progressive and equal we are. But scratch the surface and most of us still really believe that childrearing is a woman's role in life. Breadwinning, and pretty much everything except doing childcare and associated tasks, is a man's.

And that's exactly how we continue to organise our lives. That's how governments shape the world of work. It's how the NHS, public services and schooling are delivered. And it's how media, advertising, most parenting experts, our employers and even our dear parents tell us we should go about it. Fathers who try to split childrearing more equitably, particularly care of babies, remain the freakish exception.

Yet ask most people with children what they want out of life, and the new fatherhood myth prevails. Most fathers think they should spend more time with their children, and most working men say they want to spend more time with their families. But their actions to actually do so are at best muted. Childcare is still hugely, overwhelmingly done by women. Working fathers most often work full-time, working mothers most often work part-time.

Men with children spend more hours at work than those who don't, and this can't simply be explained away by the need to earn more. The difference is most pronounced in senior and managerial jobs, likely to come with a fixed salary. One in three fathers doesn't even take the two weeks' paternity leave he is legally entitled to, and the same proportion had already ruled out taking the new 2011 entitlement to a share of 26 weeks' parental leave before it was even introduced. There's no indication men are likely to take any larger share of their new right to parental leave when it is introduced in 2015.

Even in the much-trumpeted Scandinavian countries, where employment legislation is constructed to enable and encourage more fathers to care for children (with the aim of supporting children and families better overall), men don't use their voluntary entitlement. In Iceland, Sweden and Norway men do take the leave that only they can use, but when it comes to sharing leave with their female partner, men take only a tiny minority.

It's not just who does childcare and who goes out to work where inequality persists. Peek behind the curtains of domestic life and a familiar pattern emerges. Overwhelmingly it is still women who do the hard slog of childrearing. Not the high-visibility nappy change, the weekend visit to the park or the occasional school drop-off, but the daily ticking-over of shopping for food, buying clothes, making and attending doctor's appointments, buying presents, washing, changing sheets, preparing meals and more. Ironically it is among childless couples that housework is most likely to be shared.

In the weeks following a baby's birth, men frequently excuse themselves from the same bedroom as the infant so their sleep isn't disturbed. After all, *they* have a full day's work ahead. Only a third of couples report taking it in turns to get up for a new baby during the night.

All of this enduring inequality is despite clear and overwhelming evidence that fathers' involvement in their children's lives is not only better for their children, but also for their marriage and even for their own jobs. Children whose fathers are actively involved in their care are likely to have better development on almost every level. They are more sociable and stable, have better educational attainment and are less likely to be involved with the police. Meanwhile, relationships between married couples are more positive when the father is more actively involved with the children. And fathers who work flexibly enjoy better health, are less stressed and have better relationships with colleagues.

If men aren't following up their stated desire to do more childrearing with actually doing it, what is going on?

This book explores some of the reasons why inequality endures. It offers both anecdotal and research evidence on why men playing a fairer or even equal role in childcare remains a must-get-round-to rather than a must-do-now priority for most families.

The UK's working culture and employment legislation should certainly shoulder some of the blame. Like women on maternity leave, men are paid less than the minimum wage when they take statutory paternity leave. Both women and men only have a right to *ask* for flexible working and reduced hours, not a right to be *granted* them. As I'll argue, the coalition government's new 'family friendly' policies, due to come into force in 2015, will actually do very little to change the status quo of the mother as primary childcarer.

Maternity, midwifery, early years and public services for parents are also at fault. From the sonographer's chair, via the maternity ward, to the health visitor's practice, men are regarded as add-ons at best, actively not welcome at worst. Mums themselves, particularly when united outside the pre-school and nursery gates, do little to make involved dads feel part of their world, while there are few positive role models of engaged, active and equal fathers in the media, among politicians or public figures.

These are just some of the deeply ingrained social norms, expectations and structures that continue to offer crucial barriers to men playing an equal role in the care of their children, many and more of which I cover in the chapters that follow.

But there is another fundamental reason for this inequality that's often ignored. The truth is that most men just don't want to do it.

It's not just unfriendly maternity services, unthinking women at playgroups, lazy parenting guides, narrow-minded government policies, or even outdated employment practices that are excluding men from playing a more equal role. It is men themselves.

The rest are all undoubtable barriers, but they also offer a very convenient excuse for men to avoid what most women know, but only rarely admit. Childrearing can be amazing, satisfying, incredible and stimulating. But it is very often also boring, unrewarding, frustrating, disappointing, messy, ugly, exhausting and depressing all at the same time. Childrearing involves personal, career, ambition and financial sacrifices that most men simply aren't willing to make, yet have always been expected of women.

Culturally we're told that men go to work, and women stay at home. The tide is often so strong that it's far easier for both men and women to swim with it than against it. So men avoid the hard slog (and miss out on many of the rewards) of childrearing. The mother fulfils her expected role of primary parent, with the father mainly as *helper*.

Men still massively dominate government, parliament, the media and the private sector, and they dominate the management of the public sector, trade unions and even charities. In our homes and in society at large, men easily have the power to bring about a more level playing field, and very quickly. But we don't, because in our own homes and workplaces, as well as in our politics and public life, it is not in our interests to do so. It's not even on our agenda.

The strong cultural presumption that childcare is what women should *do,* and even a powerful lobby of organisations, books and websites that seek to maintain what they regard as a unique and exclusive bond between mother and baby, only serves as further excuse for couples to maintain the status quo.

Of course, every family thinks they have a special case. *Equality in childcare is great in theory, and yes everyone should be doing it, but it just wouldn't work in my situation.* "It's alright for you," I've heard many times. "I'd love to be equal and spend more time with my kids, but my industry, my job, my situation, my income, my location, my hobbies, my [insert-really-good-reason-here] means I *just can't*."

This is a book about how men just *can*. In it I tell the story of my own journey towards equal parenting, and my slow realisation that my token one-day-a-week of childcare was not fair. And not enough. From the day I started rubbing anti-stretch-mark cream into my wife's small but slowly growing belly, Sarah and I were committed to equally sharing all childcare-related tasks, even those you might at first think impossible for a man.

In fact, because we were one of the first couples in our friendship group to have a baby, I didn't even realise other men didn't play an equal role when it came to children. I just merrily did my fair share, thinking that's what blokes did. When I started to see what other men were doing – or not doing – it became clear I could have got away with far less. But I was already used to it, and once you're used to it, you just carry on, don't you?

Still, at work it took time for me to admit my own special case – running my own hectic business with five full-time employees and another four regular freelancers – wasn't special enough to stop me working equal hours to my wife. And as I watched her despair at a once high-octane, highly rewarding life as a television documentary producer turning to nothing, I was forced to ask myself some difficult questions: what sacrifice have I *really* made for the children we decided to have together? What commitment to my wife, her happiness and her career have I made? Two-and-a-half days a week it was to be, whether I liked it or not.

This book aims to show parents the how and why of a fairer parenting deal. I hope it provides inspiration to those who would like to do it, evidence for those who need to be convinced it is right and possible, argument for those who aren't convinced it's a problem, and practical ideas for those who just don't know how to do it. And to women who choose to use the book to beat something a little closer to

equality out of the men in their lives, please be my guest. I
wish it was in hardback.

In recent other books on gender, equality and parenting,
it has been very strongly and convincingly argued that
legislation needs to be updated, government policy needs to
change, the NHS and public services need to be overhauled,
and societal attitudes need revising. You'll find me making
exactly the same case in the pages that follow. But you'll also
find me calling on men in particular to do more themselves to
bring about parental equality. Men need to act out the change
we ought to be looking for. If we demonstrate a different way
of doing things, in our workplaces, social circles, communities
and families, even despite legislative unfairness and societal
pressures to maintain the status quo, others will follow. The
wheels will turn, and an enduring change will be created.

It can be bloody hard. I have no illusions about that.
Who wants to stand up and be the exception? Particularly
when it means spending more hours of your life elbow-deep
in whatever material your child's body has most recently
decided to discharge. But a fairer share of the work will
bring with it immense personal, family and social benefits
too important to continue to pass up. To be the change,
though, men have to want it first. That's by far the toughest
challenge: convincing men that a fairer deal is something
they should even desire.

Much of the debate about equality in parenting so far has
been led by women.[1] The debate can be too easily brushed
off as *just more moaning feminists who don't understand what
being a chap is really about*. The conspicuous absence of men's
voices in this whole area pretty much reinforces my key
argument: where are the blokes calling for parental equality
and fairness to happen? Where are the blokes showing how
equality is done?

You're in a pub with your family and there's a nappy that needs changing. Being the good new father you dutifully head off with the change bag slung over the shoulder, a smouldering of approval from the mums and grans in the pub as you trundle past their table with a slightly whiffy but still incredibly cute bundle of baby in your arms. But when you get to the loos, the only baby-change is behind the door marked *Ladies*. Do you retreat sheepishly back to your brood, hand over the baby to its mum and hold up your hands apologetically? You tried, after all.

Or do you squat?

1

The new fatherhood myth

SO HAVE YOU seen this new father knocking around the place?

I'm sure you'd recognise him. They have his picture in the papers every other week, in the family, personal finance and women's sections. Even the business section these days. The photo usually has him in the foreground, kneeling over a perfect naked baby lying on a pristine sheepskin rug, loving beaming smiles shared between the two. In the background, always just out of focus, is Mum: all power-suit, power-heels and breadwinner briefcase, heading for the door.

You must have seen him about. He's the thin one with the bright eyes, the sexy five o'clock shadow and the chizzled chin. The one wearing the beautifully turned-out tight white T-shirt, stretched over broad shoulders and a rack of firm, rippled abs.

What about his baby, surely you've seen her? She's got a cherub-like gleaming face tucked under a frilly bright white

hat. Her JoJo Maman Bébé blue dungarees perfectly matched
with light blue socks and the cutest matching booties. Not
that she needs shoes, because she's cosily tucked up in the
deep purple limited-edition Bugaboo, with darling multicoloured baby-sense stimulation toy waving gently over her
as she sleeps.

You know the new father. He's the one always bouncing
the baby in his muscular arms, while running barefoot along
the surf's edge, throwing his head back with a massive smile,
simply basking in the love of the daughter he's so lucky to
spend his every waking hour with. You mean you haven't
seen him? I haven't either but, you know, its kinda busy out
here. What with looking after the kids and everything.

Maybe I missed him that time I was in Loafers cafe on
Culver Street in Colchester, Essex. That time when I brushed
some uneaten sandwich off my son's trousers to find it was
actually a pile of his shit, and then I noticed there was more
shit erupting over the top of his waistband in a non-stop
faecal volcano, even as he blissfully chomped away on a
panini. Maybe I missed that guy when I grabbed a greasy
serviette from under my own sandwich and bent down to
pick up my own son's shit from the café floor before anyone
noticed. And then tucked it in my rucksack to deal with later.

Or maybe that guy passed by me in the aisle at Sainsbury's
that time when Erin was swinging off the front of the trolley
and knocked over an old lady with a walking frame. That
time when Reid plucked colourful shiny things from the
shelves to throw in the trolley quicker than I could remove
them, and we got bleeped by the security gate because there
were undeclared items he'd tucked away in the nappy bag.

Or perhaps I missed him that time in Tesco when I
got a call over the PA system to come collect my lost and
crying daughter, only I couldn't get past the checkouts to

the customer service desk because I had a trolley, with Reid jammed into the front, full of baby wipes, Calpol, Tiny Tots toothpaste, porridge oats and baby rice that I hadn't yet actually paid for.

But I'm sure he's around, that guy. In your city. Down your street. In your local library. Merrily enjoying his new dadness without a care in the world. After all, there's a growing trend for men, this breed of new fathers, to look after babies during the day. A growing number of men are "swapping the pinstripe for the pinny" while the women in their lives go out to work. It must be true. Bill Turnbull said it on BBC Breakfast.

Oh how newspapers and daytime TV shows love the idea of a *growing trend*. Particularly in the Sunday newspaper supplements, breathless journalists ascribe the growing-trend label to everything from men having botox to churchgoers munching biscuits during services, to couples hiring a professional photographer to capture the glorious and beautiful throes of labour and delivery.

And nowhere is this growing-trend journalism more at home than on the subject of men doing what was once regarded as a woman's role.

> *"Daddy stays at home, but Mummy has flown the nest: There is a growing trend of women handing over childcare to their men"*[1]

> *"Number of women who are family's main breadwinner soars as husbands left holding the baby"*[2]

> *"There is a new wave of dads emerging who are wheeling buggies, changing nappies and reaping the benefits and pains of hands-on parenthood.*[3]

*"The number of fathers giving up work to look
after their children is on the increase."[4]*

All of which would be great news for men, their children
and their wives (or partners★), if it was actually true. You see,
since I trained as a journalist I feel confident in saying there
really does seem to have been a growing trend for journalists
to not bother with things like evidence or statistics, and just
to write 'growing trend' or 'more and more' because it's a
simple, painless way to start a feature or TV segment. It
means: hey, I just noticed something that I find interesting,
or I've just been sent a press release that says it, and I need
to file 1,200 words and I daren't check the stats just in case
I find out that my neatly observed trend isn't actually true.

"Now that's scientific fact," as comedian Chris Morris
duped DJ Neil Fox into saying on spoof documentary *Brass
Eye*. "There's no real evidence for it, but it is scientific fact."

You see, the problem with the phrases 'growing trend'
and 'more and more' is that they're so unspecific. When, for
example, did this growing trend start? Because, compared
with the middle ages, men really do have something of
the feminist about them. Since the time of Richard the
Lionheart, there really has been a growing trend for men
to take care of the children. But there's also been a growing
trend for them not to kill each other with swords, or for
men to brush their teeth, work in offices, travel on trains,
eat Kentucky Fried Chicken and play darts.

★ *To save me having to write, and you having to read, the clumsily constructed wife/
partner compromise throughout, I've plumped for using 'wife' and 'partner', as well
as 'husband' and 'partner', pretty much interchangeably in this book. It makes
no difference if you're married or not, or even whether you use these terms or not:
my arguments are the same. I hope you get the general gist that I mean men and
women in a couple. The times when I do mean same-sex couples, I make it clear.*

What's the timescale here, guys? Did this amazing growing trend start last week? A couple of years ago? Since the London Olympics (British identity's year zero)? Since the Eighties? Since Joseph strolled around Nazareth carrying Jesus in a BabyBjörn?

If more and more dads are doing childcare during the day, or picking their kids up from school, or getting in touch with their feminine side, or making jam and baking bread, or throwing pickled gherkins at each other's bottoms, exactly when did this trend start?

Here's exactly what this particular man wants to know about a growing trend: when was it, exactly, that men weren't doing it? When did they start doing it? When, then, did more men do it? Then more men still? And are they still doing it now? And how many men weren't, then were, then still are doing it?

That's what 'more and more' men means, and that's what a 'growing trend' is. One of the earliest, and perhaps today more controversial, rules we rookie journalists were taught was that there should be no growing trends, more and mores, rising numbers of, or massive increases in, unless they were backed up by, you know, figures. Some numbers. A bar chart perhaps. Or a graph, like you used to draw at school showing how tall cress had grown in an eggshell. The kind of graph we all learned to construct when we were getting our heads around such lofty and complex scientific concepts such as 'growth' and 'time passing'. A graph with a big thick red line going up, up, up, like a newspaper cartoon's way of showing a fat cat banker raking in the profits.

A growing trend isn't some north London freelance suddenly noticing that a couple of their north London friends have started doing something edgy and interesting, and wouldn't that make a feature for *The Guardian* family supplement?

How about a game of new fatherhood bingo? Five points for every phrase – or variation of it – contained in a newspaper article, or TV or radio news report, about fathers doing a fairer share of childcare. Enjoy an extra point if it's in the headline, plus a bonus if that media piece also contains the phrases 'growing trend', 'more and more' or 'a growing number':

> *"Left holding the baby"*

> *"Daddy does daycare"*

> *"Swapping the pinstripe for the pinny"*

> *"When Mum becomes breadwinner"*

> *"When Dad plays Mum"*

> *"Mum's the word for dads who do childcare"*
> *(uhhh, pleeeze!)*

> *"Domestic God"*

> *"Traded his [insert work related item here: drill/briefcase/flipchart] for a nappy/bottle/ babygrow, etc. …"*

> *"Having it all"*

> *"Mr Mum"*

> *"Who's wearing the trousers now?"*

Even a cursory understanding of the statistics shows the breathlessly claimed 'growing trend' for 'more and more' men to care for their children is not what it seems. There has indeed been a very small increase in stay-at-home dads over the last decade, and a minuscule growth in fathers working part-time. But the numbers are tiny compared with what journalists and fathers' campaign groups would have us believe. I'll get to the actual figures in a moment, but let's take a look at some of the ways the new fatherhood myth is propagated.

The journalist may have observed a growing number of men with children at the park during the day. What they might have missed is that unemployment among men has been increasing too. There are more men with their children, because there are more men not working. They might as well kick around the park, pushing their preschoolers on the swings, because they're not doing much else right now.

In a world of strong employment, it is likely that there will be a number of enlightened and progressive men who sacrifice their career to look after their children. A small but solid proportion of men doing childcare. Whether there is paying work available or not, these chaps are going to do childcare while most other men get on with the glorious work that a booming economy has provided.

In a world of poor employment, these same enlightened and progressive men will still make up the bulk of male child carers, and they may be joined by a few more dads who take on the role because now they have time. But there will also be a large number of out-of-work dads who remain resolute that childcare has nothing to do with them. More men out of work, many more men available to do childcare – but only a slight proportional increase in those who actually do. Hardly a new fatherhood revolution.

PR companies with something to sell, as well as father-hood organisations, make much of the claim that there are now huge numbers of men doing childcare, and many thousands more are desperate to do it but are being prevented. But just a little analysis shows how weak these claims can often be.

According to the Fatherhood Institute, nearly a quarter of dads of under-fives are solely responsible for childcare at some point during the week.[5] That could of course be for just five minutes a week, and is hardly a growth in stay-at-home dads or men taking over the childcare from their wives. Nearly half of fathers of school-age children provide care before or after school. How often and for how many days a week, isn't revealed. And what were all these dads doing before their kids went off to school for most of the working day?

Imprecise statistics that don't tell the whole truth can easily be used by busy or lazy journalists, not to mention those with an axe to grind, to conveniently jump to the wrong conclusions about men and parenting, because that makes a better story.

The Institute says 1% of biological fathers are in 'sole charge' of babies for more than 30 hours per week. But again, it doesn't say whether that's overnight, during the day or while the woman is at work. And that's still only one father in every 100 couples. A number we're supposed to be proud of?

In families with three- and four-year-olds, 4% of the fathers do the 30 hours' 'sole charge'. Hardly staggering numbers for male babycarers, and even on Fatherhood Institute figures definitely not a breed of new fathers challenging mothers for childcare supremacy.

Let's go now to the private sector. According to a survey carried out by telephone and internet provider BT and widely covered in the media, "One in two fathers (49%) say they do the majority or an equal share of the childcare."[6] One in two! Half of all dads do an equal share or even more than mothers? Tuck your placards away, girls, the battle is won!

Except for one thing. Where the hell are these guys?

I live in a pretty middle class, fairly progressive area of the south east of England. And I don't see them anywhere. I should see blokes all around me, happily ferrying their kids around, taking toddlers to playgroups, doing the school run. By BT's reckoning, sing along at the local library should have at least 10 men winding the bobbin up with their toddlers. Yet, out of 40 or so regular adult attendees, it has me. Even if we allow the idea that men feel intimidated at playgroups, this army of male child carers should be out there in town, shopping in Sainsbury's, at the park, at the swimming baths, at the library, at the school gates with their babies picking up siblings. But they're just not there.

I see women. I see lots of women. Women with push-chairs. Women with kids on the bus. Women in groups at coffee shops. Women at toddler groups. Women in Tesco with two kids stuffed side by side in the front of the trolley. But chaps? Nope.

The figures quoted by the Fatherhood Institute, let alone BT, indicate I should see at least a few other dads knocking around the place from time to time. Yet fathers with young children during the week – outside of journalist-filled north and west London at least – remain a rare and amazing sight, so strange that when we do spy each other we avoid eye contact because we're so embarrassed by our uniqueness.

Unless, of course, we're to believe that those male child-carers tend to keep their children safely hidden indoors, behind closed curtains, away from the scary world of women with Quinnys. And if so, perhaps a more urgent issue we should be discussing is the thousands of children who are locked up like Rapunzel by their carers (all of whom happen to be men), unwilling to share them with the rest of society.

I don't even see many dads of school-age children at the drop-off. Certainly more than I see around town during the day, but nowhere near the numbers these statistics would lead us to expect. I have around 10 close male friends, and all of us are pretty liberal, middle-class guys. Not one of them – not one – does an equal or majority share of childcare. Only one does anything even remotely close: he takes one day off every two weeks to do childcare – at least if he's not too busy at work. In fact, now I think about it, I've never even met one other man who does an equal share of childcare during working hours. Have you?

Perhaps there's something wrong with the statistics. Ask yourself right now: are you an equal parent? If you're a man, would you say you were an equal dad? Ask any man if they do their fair share of childcare, and there's a good chance they'll say "yes". I go to work, I come home, I give Mum a break by taking the kids for an hour, I help put them to bed most nights; fair's fair. I'm equal. Hey, maybe I do more than she does.

But what about the man who works part-time, exactly the same number of working hours as his wife? That's me, and I'd like to claim to be equal too. I do the same number of childcare hours as she does, I put them to bed the same number of times, I cook their tea the same number of times. I do the washing, the dressing, the doctor's appointments, just as often as she does. Which of us is right? Some of us, it seems, are more equal than others, and these surveys may well be missing the point.

It's very easy to say your parenting is equal, and almost necessary if you feel the question or survey is challenging your family situation. But unless someone gives us a definition of what equal or fair parenting is, the figures are bound to get skewed by self-definition. Or else skewed by whatever point or product the questioner is trying to sell with their survey.

In her excellent US-focussed book *Halving It All: How equally shared parenting works*, Francine Deutsch put out a call for case studies of equal parents to interview. She received submissions from couples who defined themselves as equal, but surprised the researchers by actually being far from it.

"A surprisingly high number of couples we talked to by phone claimed to divide the care of children 50:50," she writes. "When we investigated further with questions about specific tasks, their estimates changed... many of the couples revised their estimates to more realistically reflect the disproportionate share shouldered by mothers."

Many fathers who responded to the call for shared parenting case studies worked full-time, while their wives stayed at home. Some did no housework or babycare. Some provided *help* to the wife, but had never looked after the child alone. And they claimed to be doing an equal share.

One interviewee who later became an equal parent looked back on when his child was first born, when he was working long hours, and admitted: "If you had asked me at the time, I would have said that Donna and I are equal... I truly believed in my mind that I thought we were equal."

And maybe I'm in the same boat. Rather boastfully, I claim throughout this book to be an equal father, and I compare other people's experience to my own. Many are not equal, compared with my own definition. But whose definition should win? Whether you're a man or a woman, ask yourself if it's you or your partner who is more likely to:

Do around half of the childcare during the week,
working hours included.

Empty the potty of poo and wee, giving it a wipe,
then offering same to your children's backsides.

Prepare breakfast, lunch, dinner and snacks for
the children.

Buy clothes, shoes, medicines for the children.

Arrange and go on play-dates, children's parties
and group outings with your children.

Participate in songs, games and mealtimes at above
children's dates and parties.

Buy presents, thank-you cards, wrap and write
them, and send them on behalf of your children.

Arrange childcare, school and outing drop-offs, and
carry them out.

Write letters to said school and your children's teachers,
and fill in the countless forms and permission slips.

Attend health check-ups, immunisations, dental
and doctor's appointments with your children.

Gather, scrub stains from, wash, dry, iron, sort, fold
and put away your children's clothes.

Sew name labels into same.

Tidy your children's bedroom, throw out old toys, buy new ones.

Change your children's sheets, wash them, iron them (iron them?!) and replace.

Parents behind the website EquallySharedParenting.com publish a comprehensive checklist, far fuller than the list above. It urges parents to sit down and complete it together to really interrogate how equal they are. It's supposed to be a starting point for a discussion (for which read *blazing row*) about how to create a fairer deal. And do you know what? I fail badly. When I read their list for the first time, I realised there was a whole swathe of childcare I wasn't even consciously aware of, and which my wife just did automatically – she wasn't aware she was doing it either. And even setting out the short list above makes me think there's way more I could and should be doing.

All of which is not to attempt to make even the most progressive fathers feel inadequate. Rather, it's to show how deeply ingrained the woman-as-childcarer role is, how easily men overlook non-obvious childcare tasks, and how claims of a growing trend of equal dads simply don't bear out when put to the test.

By the way, I know what you're thinking. There are loads of male jobs that women don't do, so women aren't equal either. I don't see many women putting up shelves, or filling skips, or clearing the gutters, or fixing the dripping tap, or lifting fridge-freezers so the man in their life can vacuum underneath it. Or for that matter, driving the car when the family goes on holiday. Men do male jobs, and those jobs offset the female jobs that just happen to be the soft, cuddly ones that include looking after, cooking for, and cleaning up after the kids. Equals–pequals; we're doing our share.

What's missing here is the question of need. That shelf can wait, the tap can keep on dripping. But when your child needs to poo, or to eat, to have its bed changed or to be taken to the doctors, there's no option, there's no "I'll get round to it". A trip to the dump can be put off: clearing up a child's dump can't.

When we have children, we commit ourselves to a job of work with timescales, deadlines and demands that our working life has never dared put upon us. There have been times when my two kids have been naughty, tired and whiney, jumping on the sofa and poking and punching each other, that have brought me to absolute unadulterated desperation. I just can't do this anymore, I've thought and even howled out loud at them. I've been so fed up of them that I've wanted to just walk away, close the front door and leave them to holler and wail by themselves. Destroy the house, I don't care. But however much you want to walk away, you just can't. You have to stick it out. Whatever demons appear to have possessed your little angels, you have to care for them. You have to continue the hard slog of parenting, the thankless job of childcare. There's no choice. I've never felt that way about mowing the lawn.

Despite the thousands of terabytes of information on the web about how to look after children, and the millions of trees' worth of books written on the subject, it seems to come as a surprise that childcare includes all these extra jobs on top of the cuddling and cooing and the occasional nappy change or bottle feed. With men most often safely installed back at work, women learn about these extra jobs the hard way – as they go along. The man remains none the wiser, or if he does find out about them, chalks them up on the "her" side, offsetting his getting the MOT renewed.

Most astounding is that we parents spend nine months waiting for our little treasure to be born, discussing the colours of the bedroom walls, who to tell in what order, what to call our bundle of joy and what kind of future we hope they'll have, without actually discussing in our hazy pre-labour enthusiasm: what might it actually take to raise and nurture a small human being? What's the job description? And, well, who is actually going to do all this stuff?

★ ★ ★

It's a common lament from men: they'd love to see their children more and play a more hands-on role, but work itself and attitudes at work towards fathers, well, they just get in the way. And there is no doubt at all that most men *do* want to do more of the childcare, or at least to spend less time at work so they can be with their kids. Survey after survey puts this high on men's agenda.

A YouGov poll for the Equality and Human Rights Commission revealed that 42% of parents disagreed that childcare is the mother's primary responsibility (though a third did agree).[7] Nearly half of fathers said they don't currently spend enough time with their children, and over half said they spent too much time at work. Only 16% of fathers said work should come before their children. A whopping near two-thirds of men, according to the poll, thought that fathers (in general) should spend more time caring for their children.

The charity Working Families reports that a full eight out of ten full-time working men say they would like more time with their families.[8] The Fatherhood Institute says a third of fathers would take a pay cut to spend more time with their children, and recounts reams of similar statistics on fathers wanting more time with the kids and less at work.[9]

But there is a clear and demonstrable difference between men thinking the mum-as-childcarer role is old fashioned, and them doing anything to buck that trend. And there is a clear and demonstrable difference between men saying they want to spend more time with their children and less time at work, and them actually doing it.

This is the biggest fallacy of all in the new fatherhood myth: the equation between men *liking the idea of* being a more actively involved father, and *actually being* an actively involved father. Yes, the desire is definitely there. But whatever the journalists say about growing trends, it is not being backed up by more fathers taking more paternity leave, more parental leave, by working flexibly, part-time or even giving up their work completely. Men aren't even spending that much time with their kids outside of working hours, and certainly not as much as mothers are. The myth makes a good story, but once again it's just not true.

So, where does this breathless picture of the new father-hood come from? And does it matter? Certainly there's an element of zeitgeist journalism at play here. Lifestyle writers pluck a chance or one-off piece of news from public life – David Beckham wears a sarong, Tom Daley receives abusive tweets, Lindsey Lohan gets thrown out of a party, Prince Harry plays naked billiards – and they extrapolate that public one-off into a growing trend for us all to do the same.

Usually, they find a couple of case studies of other people who've done that same thing, they then get a university expert to say it's ever so interesting that people are doing it, and they write a witty signoff summing it all up as zeitgeist social observation. Bingo, there's your feature written. And sure, it makes for a few column inches and a mildly interesting read on a Saturday afternoon. We buy this stuff, we read it, so what?

More insidious is what award-winning investigative journalist Nick Davies has dubbed 'churnalism': the tendency for lazy or overworked journalists to take PR company guff and effectively rearrange the paragraphs in their press release, then pass it off uncritically as a comment piece, or worse a news story. In our celebrity-obsessed, content-hungry society, journalists have neither the time nor inclination to examine whether the PR company spin or their figures are biased or even true. They just churn out the stories as the press releases come in because it's easier and cheaper that way. Stories on new fatherhood clearly show churnalism at work.

"Dads take on childcare duties in one in seven UK households," heads up the press release from Aviva. "Dads are the main childcare provider in one in seven (14%) UK households with dependent children...The study suggests at least 784,000 men in the UK, now take on the role of the 'primary parent'."

Aviva is an insurance company. A company whose PR consultants have – and good luck to them, that's their job – carried out a survey they hope will, when covered by the media, encourage more families to take out life insurance.

"We'd encourage every family to consider the 'what ifs' to make sure they're financially protected, just in case the unexpected should happen," the press release continues.

"Aviva offers £10,000 worth of free life cover to new parents, per parent, per child up to their first birthday."

And the media duly do what Aviva hoped: reproduce the story as revealing a new social trend.

> *"Stay-at-home dads on the up: one in seven*
> *fathers are main childcarers," says The Guardian.*[10]

> *"The rise of the stay-at-home dad: One in seven*
> *families now have father as primary carer for*
> *children," says the Daily Mail.*[11]

> *"Breadwinning wives lead to more*
> *househusbands," says The Telegraph.*[12]

> *"FATHERS are the main child carers in one in*
> *seven UK homes," gasps The Sun.*[13]

Aviva has been doing the same survey year after year, and year after year our media cover the story in the same impressed terms. In 2010 the BBC's Michael Blastland pointed out how Aviva's annual survey might not be quite what it was cracked up to be (though only after BBC News online had already published an uncritical story about the survey, "Stay-at-home fathers 'up 10-fold'"):[14]

"Here's a general rule of statistical reporting: if it sounds amazing, don't expect it to be true... Aviva compared a wrong proportion drawn from official figures in 2000 with an extrapolation of a small survey today, based on different criteria."[15]

Yet Aviva continued to use the same data source and the same methodology in 2011. Aviva's press office never responded to my request to provide the actual data on which their story is based. But it's not just Aviva. Other companies know too that they're onto an easy win by spinning the new fatherhood myth in their favour.

"Two thirds (67%) [of fathers] don't think their employers have sufficient family-friendly policies," according to a press release from BT, which arguably has more than a passing interest in promoting flexible working from home – what with all the internet connections and telephone-conferencing facilities they could provide.

"Three quarters of dads polled wish they spent less time working and more time with their kids," says a release from discount website savoo.co.uk that helpfully reminds readers it "is offering some great deals on cheap weekends away that won't break the bank, and experience days out that'll get the family laughing together and help fathers feel really appreciated and part of the family. "

"Modern Day Father downs tools for cookbooks and dusters says new survey," this one from notonthehightstreet.com and released to coincide with Fathers' Day.[16] And how to recognise what a great dad he has evolved into by doing all these modern jobs? "We have unique gifts that suit all fathers and capture how much he really means to you," says CEO Holly Tucker.

But let's be fair. If we media consumers didn't gulp down this stuff in huge, greedy chunks, the PR companies wouldn't use it, and the journalists wouldn't write it. We love this stuff. We easily swallow the idea of the new fatherhood because it makes a great story. We just lap up the unusual and the quirky. Did you know bananas can cure cancer? Wow, a monkey that glows in the dark. Oooh, look over there, a man looking after a baby. Isn't it all just, amaaazing? That we still find a man with a baby quirky just goes to show how rare a sight it really is.

The new fatherhood story also prevails because it makes us men and women feel good about ourselves. It's not like in our grandparents' day, when women were chained to the sink and the bed, men went down t'pit to scrape coal with their bare hands, and all real blokes finished each day off

downing 15 pints of warm stout and smoking a fistful of
Lambert and Butlers. Look, everyone, the men of today are
soft, and sensitive. They moisturise. They care for children,
and know how to change nappies. They hug and hold hands
with their kids, and take them to school. I saw one wiping
a child's nose the other day, it was so sweet. Haven't we all
progressed so much since those barbarian times? Well, thank
goodness for that.

This media representation of a growing trend in super-
sensitive new fathers lets men and women off the hook.
And it prevents most of us from taking any serious action
– personally or politically – to actually give equal or fairer
parenting a fighting chance. Actually, the new fatherhood
myth offers the impression there is no battle to be fought.
If there are so many equal dads out there already, then
society is already progressing towards equality on its own.
It doesn't need persuasion or action to get it over the
hump. And it certainly doesn't need me to do anything.
There are all these other blokes who are blazing the trail,
probably because they're freelances or unemployed or gay
or something. I fully support them, of course, but my work
is a bit different, I don't think I'd be good at childcare, and
it wouldn't work for my family anyway, but, God, you've
got to admire them for doing it. I'm right behind them.
Jolly good show.

Or worse still, the new fatherhood myth convinces many
dads that they are already equal, that they themselves are
indeed one of this growing breed of new fathers, already
doing their fair share. So there's nothing they need to do
anyway. A lack of proper definitions or understanding of
what equality means, coupled with dodgy use of statistics
and PR spin, leads to men and women's own assumptions
of our parental role going unchallenged.

In *Shattered: Modern motherhood and the illusion of equality*, Rebecca Asher writes of her shock that – when she had a baby – women were still expected to do the huge majority of everything to do with children and childcare. Things hadn't changed anywhere near as much as she'd thought. She, like all of us, had bought into the new fatherhood myth.

The myth lets politicians off the hook too. If you repeat something enough times – like the idea that a number of men playing an active role with their children is increasing hugely – it becomes part of the social canon: true, simply by being said again and again and again. Politicians read papers too and they being (broadly) human also casually buy into the myth that involved fatherhood is blossoming and burgeoning in its own sweet way. They then see no need to create policies that proactively promote equality in parenting. The battle is already being won, so it isn't even on their agenda. The new fatherhood myth, promoted by a media that knows we like a good story, and lapped up by consumers and politicians who find it a convenient excuse to maintain the status quo, is actually hampering the progress it so readily trumpets.

All of which brings us to a single and pretty fundamental question: according to real statistics (rather than PR guff and lazy hack churnalism), are more blokes actually looking after children, or not?

The truth is that there has been a very small rise in the number of stay-at-home dads over the last decade, and a tiny increase in the number of men working part-time, but whether those part-time blokes are looking after children isn't clear. There has been nothing even close to the avalanche of new fathers most of us have been led to assume.

The startling claims, like those made by Aviva and BT, get picked up and circulated as if they're the absolute truth simply because they're the most surprising. And they're most surprising, it turns out, because they're not actually true.

The official UK statistics tell a very different story to the surveys put out by insurance companies, voucher code websites and campaign groups. To keep this relatively readable, I hope you'll excuse my summarising here and providing the stats in more detail in the notes for this chapter.

First, the stay-at-home dad. Or as I've seen in some American publications, the SAHD. And yes, it is pronounced 'sad' – as if we needed any stronger indication of the high regard in which men that look after children are held.

The Office for National Statistics groups men who do not work at all because they look after children or the home into the category of 'economically inactive, looking after the family/home'.

In 2002, there were 190,000 men UK-wide who were classified in this way.[17] In the period August to October 2012 there were 220,000. That, indeed, is a growth. But not a massive one: just 30,000 more blokes are caring for the home now than a decade ago.

But here's the really interesting thing: when you account for the number of those men who are not actually looking after children – instead caring for an elderly relative or a relation with a disability – the number of men doing full-time childcare more than halves. It turns out that in 2002 there were really only 80,000 men looking after children full-time. Even then statisticians at the ONS were onto the fallacy of the new fatherhood myth, reporting: "Interestingly these men most commonly look after an adult or relative and do not look after children. This shows that there is very little incidence of men 'swapping roles' with the women in their household in order to fill the childcare gap left by mothers returning to work."[18]

The ONS has now stopped separating out the categories as specifically as it did in 2002, but let's make the pretty fair assumption that men today haven't suddenly stopped caring for adults or disabled relatives in any great number over the last 10 years. Given that the population is ageing and disabilities services are being cut, it might even be reasonable to assume men's care for other adults in the family has actually increased.

That means, on 2012 figures, right now the number of stay-at-home dads in the UK is actually around the 92,600 mark. That is just 12,600 more stay-at-home dads than there were 10 years ago.

But that's still not the whole story. To add to the cremation of the new fatherhood myth, only around half of *those* men are looking after children under school age. And let's face it, looking after babies and toddlers full-time is very different to being at home looking after kids who go off to school for most of the day. The number of men looking after babies and toddlers full-time has indeed increased in the last decade – by the grand total of 6,158 fathers, across the whole of the UK.

For those who are sports orientated, you'd need two-and-a-half times that many dads to have filled the 2012 Olympic beach volleyball stadium. And over 14 times that many to fill Wembley. A growing trend? Just about. A revolution in how we organise our lives when it comes to younger children? Far from it.

In comparison to that increase of 6,158 stay-at-home dads for babies and toddlers, there are now around 44,000 fewer stay-at-home mums doing babycare than there were 10 years ago. Far fewer women are doing childcare and babycare full-time, but the idea that men are coming in to replace them in huge numbers is simply fallacy. Nurseries, childcarers, grandparents and other relatives are plugging the massive gap that men haven't come in to fill.[19] Hardly able to believe the difference between the myth and the reality, I checked these figures with a researcher at the ONS. They confirmed them.

Now let's turn to part-time work. Given most parents now do at least some work, this should give us another window on the role, or otherwise, that men are playing in childcare during the working week. The Annual Survey of Hours and Earnings has followed, year by year, patterns in working hours since 1998, and they're published on the internet for all to see.[20] Unfortunately, the survey doesn't tell us what workers are doing when they're not at work, meaning we don't know whether they work part-time because of childcare or for some other reason. Nevertheless, the proportions of men and women employed full- and part-time should give us an indication of the general lie of the land. (To assume that childcare is a significant factor in men's part-time working could even to be too generous to men, given many have been forced to go part-time due to the economic crisis. But let's be generous.)

In 2001, nearly half of the workforce (48%) were men working full-time, and a little over a quarter (28%) were women working full-time. The remaining quarter was made up of part-timers: 20% women, and just 4% men.[21] Flip forward a decade, and the majority of full-time working adults are still men: 45%, compared with 28% women. The remainder is made up of part-timers: 21% women, and just a tiny increase to 6% men.[22]

To put it succinctly, and devastatingly for the new fatherhood myth, the number of full-time men has dropped very slightly in the last 10 years, while the proportion of women working full-time hasn't changed in a decade. The tiny gap left by those previously full-time men has been filled by a slight increase in both part-time men and part-time women. It seems clear: those tiny numbers of men who have gone part-time might be doing more childcare, but their doing so has not allowed women to go back to work full-time, and only led to very slightly more part-time workers of either gender.

So what about when people are asked – by the official bean counters – how much childcare they actually do? How much childcare-related stuff are men doing now, compared with what they did? Has that increased significantly?

The ONS no longer asks people what they do with their time, so the most up-to-date official data we can get about people's self-reported time spent caring for children, versus working, or doing housework, or indeed sleeping, is from 2005. But there is a 2000 version too, which means we can get a general idea of any change. (Note: you can't really draw conclusions about trends based on comparing *only* two sets of figures. Unfortunately, interim figures aren't available.)

In 2000, men reported doing 11 minutes of childcare per day as a primary activity, compared with 15 minutes in 2005.[23] (The amount seems low because it's averaged out among all men, including those without children.) Definitely an increase – one of four minutes a day. But women reported an increase too, from 28 minutes to 32 minutes per day. Another four-minute increase, but on their already more than double share. So both men and women were doing slightly more childcare in 2005 than in 2000, but for men that four minutes adds up to a bigger proportional growth on the little amount they were doing. But still, no great revolution in gender roles.

This same survey shows that men who worked part-time in 2005 actually reported doing around the same amount of domestic work (including childcare) as men who worked full-time. And those men who are unemployed did far less than either part-timers or full-timers.[24] It also showed men with children work longer hours than those without them.

Let's sum up! Based on government data, collected and analysed by the Office for National Statistics:

* There has been a tiny increase in the number of fathers looking after pre-school age children full-time over the last 10 years, but certainly not anywhere near enough to replace the women who have stopped doing it.

* Only a tiny proportion of the workforce is made up of part-time men, and their number has only very slightly increased in the last decade.

* There has been no revolution in women returning to work full-time over the last 10 years, but instead very slightly more women have been able to return to part-time work, joined by very slightly more part-time men.

* More childcare activity on average is being reported by men, but a similar increase in time doing childcare was reported by women.

In conclusion, and once and for all: very slightly more men do seem to be doing a very slightly larger proportion of the childcare. Is it a huge and startling growing trend?

Definitely not. Is it an indication of gender-role revolution? Far from it. Is it the birth of a legion of new fathers? Not for some time yet.

It is time to lay the new fatherhood myth to rest. And instead to ask: why aren't men taking on the childcare responsibility in the huge droves we've assumed or been told they are? And what's really stopping them?

2

Fathers not visitors

THE DAY MY wife went into labour for the birth of our first child was one of nervousness, excitement and anticipation. We knew it was going to happen because we had a whole afternoon's notice.

We were living in Northern Ireland at the time, where Sarah's work was then based, only moving to Essex in the south-east of England once our daughter had come along. Sarah was four days overdue and we woke that morning with a small damp puddle in the bed. Was this the much-vaunted breaking of the waters? Not so much a gush as a trickle, we decided to leave it for a few hours. We'd go get some breakfast and see what happened next.

By lunchtime there was more liquid, but still no definitive gush. Sarah called the labour department at Ulster Hospital in east Belfast, and was advised it was best to come in. If her waters had broken, the baby might be at risk of infection.

Later, still with no contractions in attendance but no definitive answer from the doctors as to whether labour had started either, it was decided an induction would be the best route. Something they would get under way later, offering us the whole afternoon together to get excited about the forthcoming experience of having our first baby. By late afternoon we were fed up of the blank waiting room walls and stole out of the hospital and across the Upper Newtownards Road to climb a low grassy hill overlooking the hospital.

Together we stood on the top, held hands and took in a panorama of Belfast as the April sun gently lowered over the harbour. This world was the one into which we were, together, about to bring a baby. Even with the sectarian flags flapping in the distance, it was a world that didn't look too bad.

We retreated to the hospital for a cuddle and an excited chat about what we were about to go through. Knowing we were enjoying each other's company as a childless couple for the last time ever, we sat there nervous, sharing, anticipating, in love. And then something really amazing happened.

I was told to go home.

Sarah's induction (requiring the painful insertion of a pessary close to her cervix) would be done once I had left. My wife would go into labour and experience the uncomfortable, then painful, then crippling, onset of contractions without me. But if I wouldn't mind leaving my number at the desk on the way out, next to the car park payment booth, they'd be sure to call me when the baby was coming.

A slap around the face. Quickly but firmly delivered. It woke us up from the hazy excitement we'd dared to share that afternoon, that we were about to have a baby *together*. This labour, and this baby, I had been told in no uncertain terms, was nothing to do with me. Now, run along to the car park and let us women get on with it.

I went away and sat in a deserted bar on Holywood High Street, supping half a Guinness and staring in turn between a pile of beer mats and my mobile phone, waiting for the call. Sarah meanwhile was crawling up the walls.

The induction took hold almost immediately after I'd left, and delivered her wave after wave of painful contractions. As the night wore on she didn't feel she could cry out because she was in an open ward full of other women, some sleeping, some writhing in their own silent torment. At just past midnight and on the way to the toilet to be sick again, her waters broke – this time for real. And as she stood there in the middle of a hospital corridor about to throw up, with a slippery pool of amniotic fluid gathering around her bare feet, I couldn't be there to reassure her, hold her hand, call over someone in a uniform to tell them what had happened, or pass her the sick bucket.

She went through the bulk of labour, the long hours of painful build up, surrounded by people but completely alone. And without me, her husband and the father of our first child who was on her way.

The call finally came about five in the morning, just after I'd switched off some early morning cheap-to-make TV show: probably the 100 Best Irish Love Songs of All Time, presented by some has-been celebrity I vaguely recognised. By the time I got to the hospital and found her labour room, Sarah was stripped from the waist down, doubled-up over her hospital bed, chuffing intermittently on the gas and air, and completely unable to speak.

"She's doing fine," the midwife said, without looking up from her notes. That was the first and only time the midwife spoke to me for the entirety of the rest of her time there.

And as night shift turned into day shift, and as my wife's labour went on, no fewer than seven midwives came and went. And only one – one out of seven – introduced herself to me. None of them told me how much progress was being made. Not once was I offered a drink, told where to find a kitchen, or even the toilets.

As my wife tried a dozen different positions to get the slightest bit of comfort, white from the pain and sky high on remifentanil, she couldn't have communicated her needs if she had wanted to. We had written a birth plan of course, but this sat under a sheet of papers next to the bed and wasn't consulted. Every time I spoke to a midwife, trying to offer our preference not to have an epidural if possible, and a caesarean only in an absolute emergency, I'd receive a pat on the head: "We'll see when the time comes," or "We'll talk to a doctor if we need to." There was my wife lying on the slab, the one with whom I'd made promises to ensure that she would have the kind of labour and birth we'd talked about. Yet I was being treated like some kind of unwanted, unneeded loiterer. A fart in a lift, that everyone wishes would go away.

And as the labour went on for more hours, midwives started talking in jargon to my wife. And she, delirious with pain and painkiller, couldn't understand a thing they were saying.

"You need to get this baby out soon," said one. "The doctors are circling."

What? The doctors are circling? Is our baby dying? Is my WIFE dying? What the HELL does that even mean? If the doctors are going to come in and cut my wife open, I want to be part of the decision. I want in. I don't care if our baby dies, I just want her to be OK. I'm the husband. Surely, the DEAL in these places, is that I GET A SAY?

The midwives meant that a doctor would eventually come in with a set of forceps and a vacuum pump. They would then yank my daughter's head out of the pelvic crevice she had stubbornly lodged herself into. But they didn't say that to me. As the sun rose again over the Black Mountain, a small nick with a scalpel and a lot of pulling and pushing eventually resulted in a pretty safe, relatively normal – if a bit gory down the business end – ventouse birth.

But from beginning to end, what was going on was kept a big secret; an ancient truth that the man wasn't to be let in on. Better for him to be confused and terrified that his wife is going to die, than to allow him into the ancient mystery of labour and birth endurance that should be known only to woman.

I now realise why our own fathers say the day their children were born was the best day of their lives. Most of them weren't bloody there. They were already celebrating in the pub.

Erin's birth wasn't wonderful, or moving, or full of joy and rapture. It was a horror movie, only with more blood and more screaming. One in which I was a co-writer and knew the ending, but in which I didn't have any plot control.

And you know what sequels to horror movies are like? When my son Reid was born, there was yet more blood, yet more gore, and yet more screaming. The same plot, and again totally out of my control. I was the one holding Sarah down on the bed to prevent her reaching for a blunt spoon and cutting our son out of her own uterus. I assumed I was in a pretty good position to suggest that maybe it was me, and not her, that was in a fit state to let the midwives know what our chosen preferences might be. Yet once again, women in uniform talked to each other and not to me.

Then at six in the morning, almost with the flick of a switch, everything changed. The room filled up with people I'd never seen before, all with concerned looks on their faces. One grabbed my wife's drip, another kicked off the brakes on the bed, and they started wheeling her out of the room.

Still raw from Erin's birth two years before, I practically stood in the way and bellowed: "Can someone, PLEASE, just tell me what is going on?" Again, it turned out to be relatively routine. We had been in a birthing suite – all exercise balls, cloth hammocks and multicoloured floor mats – and she was being transferred to a labour room, where emergency equipment would be on hand if needed. Doctors would come along with a set of forceps and a vacuum... and well, you know the rest.

I admit I had a little tantrum. But I wouldn't have stamped my feet so hard had someone engaged and communicated with me as we went along. Finally, Reid was safely born. Sarah was stitched up for the second time and we had a private moment together to smile, and cry, and wonder what the hell just happened. Then a midwife popped her head round the door, smiled beamingly at my wife and asked if she would like a cup of tea. Which was lovely. I suppose I could have made one for her, as well as one for me, if only they'd told me where the kitchen was.

If my wife had had a heart condition, an appendicitis or cancer, doctors, surgeons and nurses would have calmly explained to both of us what was going to happen, gone over our options together, offered us both information and perhaps pastoral support, and I might even have been given a cup of coffee while she was being attended to. But because the lump of flesh to be extracted from my wife's body was a baby, rather than an organ or a tumour, it had nothing to do with me. Sure, I could watch if I wanted to. Maybe even hold a leg. But otherwise I would be an unwanted observer rather than a participant in the birth of my own children.

About an hour or so after Reid's birth, just as Sarah and I had recovered enough to actually speak to each other and to try our hand at getting him to latch onto her breast, something amazing happened. Visiting time was over and I wasn't a patient. I was told to go home.

★ ★ ★

The business of learning about, preparing for and actually delivering a baby is, for the most part, a closed-off women's world. Men are providers of sperm, and their only other uses before a baby is born is to join with women in some laughable breathing exercises, drive her to the hospital and go fetch the overnight bag when contractions are actually under way. I should, in all honesty, have seen it coming.

At an antenatal appointment a doctor pulled a curtain between my wife and I so she could examine her pelvis. Like the sight of her pubic hair would be alien and scary to me, her vagina something from which I had to be protected. As if her naked lower half wasn't something that I had to be at least a little familiar with in order to, you know, make a baby in the first place. I should have guessed after that time when the health visitor took my wife off into a separate room (according to standard practice) to ask if I beat her, but didn't afterwards have a quiet word with me about whether Sarah slapped me around.

Of course, in this era of the new fatherhood, midwives and labour wards have had to make half-hearted attempts to engage and involve fathers in the pre-birth and during-birth experience. Not that much of it was in evidence in the labour wards of Ulster hospital in 2008 or Colchester hospital in 2010.

In that same year – 2010 – the Royal College of Midwives published a guide to involving men in antenatal and labour care, full of useful statements blown up in 42-point font, like "It helps if an expectant father feels welcomed at the birth of his baby."[1] As well as perfectly sensible suggestions like calling a father by his actual name rather than 'Dad', offering him a seat, and putting up posters that say 'fathers welcome' at antenatal classes, the guide contains other patronising and simplistic ways to get more men involved: don't arrange ante-natal appointments that clash with football matches, or when the traffic and parking situation are likely to be bad. Perhaps scatter some men's interest magazines about the waiting room.

It was as if policy wonks at the Royal College had sat around a table with a bunch of brightly coloured pens and a flipchart entitled in bold: WHAT DO MEN LIKE? And had scribbled underneath: soccer, fast roads, magazines about fishing, cheap parking. Give them another hour and further suggestions might have included having championship golf playing in a little window on the sonographer's screen, table football in the labour ward, and a PlayStation in the waiting room. A smile and a hello would have gone a long way with me. Why not start with that?

Almost every word oozing out of the RCM makes it clear that their priority is women and *their* babies. Men's involvement is only encouraged because it benefits women and babies. That men might want and need a little support, or even respect, for their own sake is overlooked. And what if a man's desires contradict what the woman wants? That's not even worth consideration.

"There is substantial evidence of the health and wellbeing benefits from fathers being involved in their partner's maternity care," says the very first line of the RCM report. "Most women want their partners to be involved in *their* pregnancy," adds the general secretary of the RCM. (My italics).

Men are treated as visitors, rather than participants, on the maternity ward, and as such are expected to keep visitors' hours when they come to be with the mother and her baby. There is clear evidence that the presence of fathers at labour and in the period up to it leads to shorter labours, less pain reported and fewer epidural deliveries.[2] Men's presence at the birth also has a direct effect on the woman's stress levels. Yet, despite the prevailing new fatherhood myth, pregnancy, labour and birth remains something regarded as happening to a woman alone, not to a couple. Men, at most, should be encouraged to support their wives, preferably unquestioningly, obediently and silently. The pregnancy belongs to the woman, not the parents.

Now don't get me wrong. Pregnancy, labour and birth are definitely one of the few aspects of having children where inequality is hard-wired. Women's and babies' needs should absolutely be the priority, for us and for midwifery.

Labour and birth – I can testify as an observer, and my wife and countless other women will testify as active participants – is likely be one of the most intense, horrifying, stressful and downright painful experiences women will ever go through. Men absolutely should be there for the support and assistance of our partners as they go through that process, and most women do want us to be there.

But that isn't and shouldn't be men's only role and value in labour and birth: to be the assistant and supporter. We are that, but we're also fathers, men, parents and human beings with our own needs, our own emotions, and our own practical needs (a cup of tea, somewhere to sit) too. Indeed, the better our own needs are acknowledged and met, from antenatal classes onwards, the better support we're likely to be for our partners anyway.

But unfortunately, that's not the approach of much of midwifery, and certainly not the medical profession, to men when it comes to labour and birth.

Janet Fyle, professional policy adviser to the Royal College of Midwives, told *Mother and Baby* magazine in 2008: "Fathers are not a priority group and don't need their own services. We mustn't lose sight of the fact that the primary concern during birth is the mother and her baby."[3]

The introduction to the RCM's latest strategic plan shows just how much of a priority involving men is for midwives: "We hope that whether you are a researcher, a midwife, a student, or a woman using maternity services, that you embrace the challenge contained in this document... that will guide and drive the quality of care that women and their babies receive."[4] Do fathers not have any part to play in embracing this challenge?

This was published well after both my children had come into the world. Then, as now, men and fathers aren't particularly on the agenda. That men are often sent home within hours of their own baby coming into the world is the clearest representation of this attitude. It is during the first five or ten hours on labour wards that women are shown by midwives how to care for their newborn, where difficult questions are addressed, and where early decisions are made. Much of that takes place while the father isn't allowed in. We're excluded from childcare, from knowledge and decisions about babycare, from day one. Actually, make that hour one.

There are a few hospitals and maternity suites around the UK where allowing men to sleep in chairs or even beds overnight has now become common practice, like across Lincolnshire and Goole Hospitals NHS Trust. The results have been overwhelmingly positive – with an average of just under half of fathers staying overnight.

In a survey cited in the RCM's own magazine, over two-thirds of men and women say that men should be allowed to stay overnight after the birth.[5] Yet most wards still send fathers packing for the night, and often during the day too, as a matter of policy. Even where men are allowed onto the labour ward out of normal visiting hours, they're rarely provided with food, drinks, somewhere to sit, or even a warm welcome and a congratulations.

We're not asking for a full bed and breakfast with a choice of smoked salmon or poached eggs. How about simply being given a comfy chair, a blanket and not being turfed out into the darkness, and away from our partners and new babies? How about professionals actually show us men how to support our partners and new babies, rather than asking us to leave and making us feel we're in the way? That way, medicine and midwifery's priority of serving women and babies the best way possible really would be fulfilled.

NHS Trusts, and the NHS as a whole, are legally obliged – under the NHS Act of 2006 and the Equality Act of 2010 – to consult all of its users, women and men, on their experiences of maternity services, and how they can be better developed to meet their needs. In February 2010, the Care Quality Commission (CQC), which oversees quality standards in maternity care, carried out the most comprehensive survey of maternity services ever to take place in England, scoring NHS trusts across the country on their maternity services' performance. Of the 25,488 maternity service users consulted for this massive benchmark assessment – which according to the CQC would be used by NHS trusts over subsequent years to improve their performance and understand maternity department users' experiences – how many were men?[6]

Not one. Men weren't even eligible to complete the questionnaire. At the end of December 2012, health minister Dr Daniel Poulter announced a new national scheme to rate the quality of NHS maternity services. Once again, it will only be the 700,000 women who give birth each year who will be eligible to feed back on the service they receive 'during one of the most stressful periods of their lives'. Men don't get a look in.[7]

In a comprehensive and detailed 2010 report on good practice in consulting maternity service users across Scotland, the Scottish Health Council mentioned the words 'men', 'man', 'father' and 'dad' a grand total of zero times.[8] Its recommendations, which talk of more effectively reaching out to 'hard to reach' groups, and the use of new technologies to consult more people, don't mention men, or that men might want their own say in how maternity services could be developed.

The only similar survey of men on maternity services for the Department of Health surveyed a grand total of 100 men.[9] It found a direct correlation between the amount of encouragement given by staff to fathers, and their levels of satisfaction with maternity services. But the survey concentrated on how happy men were about being *encouraged to be involved* in maternity services, not their satisfaction with the actual services their family received – that was asked of women, but not men, in the survey.

It was left to the Fatherhood Institute to insert a question about men's general experiences of maternity services in a wider survey on parental leave. Almost half of fathers said they had been "pretty well ignored by maternity services", with only one in four explicitly saying that hadn't been the case.[10]

At our antenatal classes, the midwives addressed the women. Men were only spoken to about how we could rub our partner's back during labour, and reminded to make sure we knew where our car keys were at all times. If my own classes were pretty rubbish at preparing fathers for the birth itself, they provided nothing at all for fathers about what happens after the baby has popped out. It was assumed that we didn't need to know, because we wouldn't be involved.

When it came to talking about the first weeks and months following the birth, it was assumed it would be the women doing the night-time nappy change, choosing the clothes, struggling with breastfeeding and howling in the early hours from lack of sleep. Boys, you might find you have to cook your own dinner from time to time, was the prevailing atmosphere. And the men in the room chuckled along as if this attitude was the fairest assessment of their capabilities.

But that's the real point. If midwives and labour wards do little to make fathers feel part of the pregnancy game, then fathers themselves are just as guilty for their own exclusion. In fact, apart from midwives there seems to be one other subset of society that believes the process of growing and then delivering a baby has very little to do with dads. It is men themselves.

At all the antenatal classes I've attended (all of them for our first child, none the second time round – exactly the same number as my wife), the few blokes that came along sat around like extras, staring at their trainers and looking bored. Not one other bloke spoke in any of the meetings. They just trooped in and out carrying their wives' bags for them, and reaching for cups of juice for the women busy fanning their faces and stroking their bloated stomachs. I took a notebook along, asked questions and for clarifications, and challenged the midwives when they recommended new-age nonsense like burning herbal joss sticks to turn our breeched daughter, and drinking raspberry tea to encourage contractions. (Neither has any scientific evidence to back it up.)

I'm sure I was regarded as some kind of interfering, mouthy male freak, yet again trying to pound women into submission, sticking his patriarchal nose into this, the last outpost of women's dominance. One of those blokes which some maternity centres aren't keen to have around, as an IPPR paper reported, because men ask too many questions, prolong appointments and essentially get in the way.[11]

(I'm sure similar attitudes prevailed at the turn of the 20th century among men, all about how interfering women were too often questioning and mouthing off about things that men knew best, such as who should have and shouldn't have the vote.)

What hope is there for equal parenting if a man who shows an actual active interest in the growing and birth of his child is regarded as an interfering, freakish, typically-male domineering troublemaker? But the truth is no other man did show an active interest. They were the car drivers, the delivers of the baby deliverers. There because they had been cajoled into it on pain of death.

I'm sorry chaps, but when are we going to grow up? We've all seen our partner's genitals before, we all know intimately what the hole our baby will come out of looks like. We know far more about sucking on nipples than most women do. We have no problem talking to each other about fannies, arses and tits, so why the coyness? Why so silent about vaginas when we're being addressed by professionals in uniform who went to college and spent months looking at full colour photographs of them? Let's talk about this stuff. Particularly when it matters, such as when the health and wellbeing of our new babies and the women we love are at stake.

And that's just the blokes who do actually turn up to antenatal appointments and classes. A huge chunk don't even put in an appearance. Less than two in three fathers attend even one antenatal appointment such as a scan or pregnancy check-up, and only one-third attend any antenatal class.[12] As one father-to-be put it to me: "Those classes aren't aimed at men, so why would I go?"

To which a simple answer would be: because all the evidence shows your partner is likely to have a longer and more painful labour if you, as birth partner, come to the labour room ignorant and unprepared. And a more complicated answer might be: because you'll learn something, get closer to your unborn baby, and it might benefit all of your family in both the short and long term.

We're back to the football fixtures again. Just as the RCM call to arrange antenatal appointments around the football is patronising, any father who wouldn't miss a match to attend one is giving off pretty clear signals about where his priorities will lie once the baby is actually born.

What do we want guys? A personal welcome to the ward from Jeremy Clarkson holding cool cans of Carlsberg and a copy of *Nuts*? To be shown to leather easy chairs by two bare-chested hot-panted beauties with 'Welcome To Antenatal' emblazoned across their tits?

This is a hospital. This is where medical things happen. This is where our babies will be brought into the world. It's not supposed to be aimed at us. Hospitals, doctors' appointments, talk about labour, sonography and even – let's be honest – the majority of the period that we actually call 'being in labour', as well as the day or so afterwards while they're both in hospital, are deathly boring. Boring, not a little icky and a hard slog. That's just the way it is. Women can't excuse themselves from it, and nor should men.

And if we are put off by a bit of foetus-induced boredom, ickyness and slog, boy are we in for a shock. Because that boredom, ickyness and hard slog of labour and birth are nothing compared with what is in store for us once our babies actually come home.

3

Why fairer parenting?

BEFORE WE REALLY get started with the reasons things can sometimes become unfair, let's tackle something which is pretty fundamental in this whole area. It's the question of: so what?

So what if men do less childcare than women, or if men put in longer hours at work while women tend to work part-time? So what if playgroups are full of mums, with only the occasional bloke poking his head in from time to time? Who cares if men are less likely to get up in the night than their wives, or change fewer nappies, or don't know how to burp an infant? Women do the bulk of the babycare, it's true. But so blummin what? What's the big deal?

After all, we've chugged along in pretty much the same way for the last hundred-thousand years or so. It was OK for our parents, and their parents before them, and we all turned out pretty much OK. Mums and dads are different. Men and women do different things. So what?

Let's start with first principles: the idea that equality and fairness are, in general, pretty good things. You know how it goes: black people and white people are the same so should have the same access to opportunities, education, legal recourse, fair treatment and all the rest. Ginger kids shouldn't get picked on, or at least no more than blonde or dark kids. You get one vote, I get one vote. My eyes may be bluer, but that doesn't mean I get to go first on the bus. So it goes with gender equality. The simple idea is that the half of the population who happen to have a winky shouldn't get better jobs, better pay, or a more or less secure family life than the other half who happen to have a twinky. All things considered, there's no insurmountable natural, physiological or psychological reason why men should get to do one kind of thing, and women should get to do another. If we can't agree on that, we probably won't agree on anything.

But the case for equal or fairer parenting isn't won or lost by appeals to its natural fairness or equality's innate virtue. I think we'll have to work a little harder than that.

Let's talk instead about our children and the benefit to them that having an active and involved father can confer, right from the earliest age. Believe it or not, this is a whole academic discipline with papers published every year on the psychosocial, physical, academic and other benefits to children of dad being around. Or not. However much we might think that it'll usually all come out in the wash, academics don't feel the same way.

Substantial father involvement from the month following birth is connected with a range of positive outcomes in babies and toddlers, including better language development and higher IQs as the baby grows up. Fathers reading to one- and two-year-olds is linked with their greater interest in books later, and time spent by fathers reading to even very young children is connected to their future reading ability.[1]

The National Child Development Study was one of those ongoing research projects that took kids born in a particular year – 17,000 kids born in England, Scotland and Wales, born in one week in 1958 to be precise – and revisited them every couple of years, to see how they were getting along. Analysis of that data clearly showed that teenagers feel closer to their fathers if their fathers were involved early with them as they were growing up. That, in turn, led to them having more satisfactory adult marital relationships themselves.[2]

Likewise children with involved fathers – defined by the research as regularly reading to their child, taking them on outings, taking an interest in their education, and doing an equal share with mothers of 'child management' – were less likely to be in trouble with the police. Where parents were separated, involved fatherhood helped protect children from later mental health problems.

Intense involvement of fathers with their very young children can offset the negative effects on children of their mothers going out to work for long periods. Meanwhile, another report showed that longer working hours among men had a negative effect on children's development because it reduced the input men could have. If fathers come home stressed from work, or are stressed by their parenting responsibilities as a result of work, that can have a negative effect on young children too.[3]

One study found that primary school children scored higher on tests of empathy if they had secure attachments to their fathers during infancy. These children were able to recognise how other children felt, and took steps to make them feel better. Infants with involved fathers tend to score higher on tests of thinking skills and brain development.[4] Across the board, fatherhood involvement is strongly related to better educational attainment among our children.

Enough! There are whole reports that outline the umpteen benefits of involved fathers with babies, toddlers, young children and teenagers. Conversely, lower levels of involvement by fathers are associated with a range of negative outcomes. It seems pretty clear that fathers' active involvement with children, even from day one, makes a significant difference to our children's overall wellbeing and educational ability. It's kind of obvious, but the closer and more involved parents (of whatever gender) are with their children, the better children fare in life. And two involved parents, it turns out, are better than one. (Actually, three caring adults is the optimum, researchers have found. Those 60s parenting communes may have been right all along.)[5]

Fairer parenting isn't only right in itself, it works better for our kids too. And if it benefits children for fathers to be actively involved from an early age, it also benefits families and men themselves more generally. Relationships are more stable between cohabiting couples if the father is involved and parents believe the father's involvement is important.[6] When men attend antenatal classes, women report feeling better supported and that their marriages are better.[7]

New mothers whose partners are supportive, well informed and involved are less likely to suffer from stress and postnatal depression, and are more responsive and sensitive to their child's needs. (Meanwhile, when women get postnatal depression, men are more likely to follow suit and get depressed themselves.[8]) Fathers who are given space to find their own way of doing things with their babies are less likely to be depressed than other fathers, and also develop a strong connection to their baby.[9]

Fathers' involvement in infant care is positively correlated with men's satisfaction with family life.[10] In a UK survey, over two in three fathers who took paternity leave said it improved the quality of family life.[11] Fathers are more satisfied with their family when they spend more time at home, and mothers are more satisfied too when they go back to work feeling fathers are doing a fairer share.[12] Mothers and fathers who operate traditional family roles experience more stress than those who share earning and caring more equitably.[13]

Despite all this positive-outcome stuff about men playing a more involved role in their young children's life, I can't help but be drawn back to the almost innate rightness of doing so anyway.

Fathers sharing childcare more fairly with women just seems like the right thing to do. When you look, for example, at how women's pay and career opportunities are held back because they do the bulk of the childcare, it makes men doing their bit an even more 'right' thing to strive for.

Just over half of women with young children are in employment in the UK, compared with nine out of ten fathers.[14] There are four times as many women working part-time than men. Professional women earn just a touch more than men until they reach childbearing age, at which point women's salaries and earning potential take a nosedive. Women with children are routinely passed over for promotion, are less likely to be recruited than men, and get paid less than men when they do return to the workforce. Less than one in five FTSE 100 directors are women, and they make up only 14% of staff on executive committees, the next rung down in corporate life. The Equal Opportunities Commission has concluded that unequal sharing of caring work between men and women is the largest single driver of the gender pay gap. There's no easy way of saying this. We think we have gender equality in the UK; we actually still have a very long way to go.

Women who have children are routinely and systematically disadvantaged in the workplace and beyond, compared not only with all men but specifically compared with men who also have children. If men with children are getting a better deal than women with children that is called inequality. That is called discrimination. And by not at least trying to do a fairer share, men are continuing to cement that discrimination in place. Indeed we're benefiting from it.

If we think that kind of inequality is kind of OK, then we should all feel free to continue on our merry little ways. But if any of this sparks even the slightest feeling of injustice or unfairness, maybe we should – women, as well as men – do something about it.

★   ★   ★

My call for a fairer deal in parenting is aimed primarily at middle-class professional couples, rather than those working in low-paid, menial, impermanent employment. By their very circumstance, men in non-professional employment are actually more likely to be looking after children during the working week than men working in professional jobs – though still in far fewer numbers than women.[15]

Working like their partners in low-paid, part-time, impermanent jobs – shelf-stacking, labouring, call centre workers, warehouse staff, cleaning – and with childcare simply unaffordable to them, working-class couples are already far more likely to revolve, chop, change and swap childcare between them just to get through the day. The part-time or shift-based nature of their work is more likely to facilitate a slightly fairer share of the childcare among working-class families. (Though still not so fair that these working-class men are ubiquitous with their kids, pounding the streets, playgroups or SureStart centres the length and breadth of the UK.)

The lower paid men and women are, the smaller the full-time pay gap between them, while in the part-time working world, women of childbearing age are actually paid slightly more than men.[16] The result is that non-professional couples have the smallest amount of choice or power to do things a different way, at least in their working lives, yet still come out slightly fairer.

In contrast, middle-class couples are less likely to share childcare during the working week. The media's BabyBjörn-wearing new father is located squarely within the middle classes, yet it is the middle classes that most betray him as a myth. Men and women in professional occupations have far more choice and power to change our working situation and to create a fairer parenting set-up, and many of us express the desire to do so. Yet we're not taking up the opportunity in any great numbers.

Middle-class men and women may find great excuses for not having a fairer childcare arrangement, but most of them are really inconveniences we're not willing to put up with. They're not real barriers we're unable to overcome. We may think our jobs don't give us a choice, but we have far more of an option to change jobs, even if it involves a slight pay and status cut, than non-professional male workers who may already be scraping the bottom of the barrel.

If we think we can't afford to take a pay cut, we can downsize our homes, cars, holidays, leisure activities, in order to better afford one. We might not want to do that, but that's not the same as being unable to. Middle-class families have much further to fall. And in that long-distance drop lie many opportunities that working-class families don't have. And many of us middle-class parents, if we're canny at negotiating with our employers, reeling in our spending and reshaping our working lives, wouldn't even need to exploit those opportunities anyway. (Indeed, as I argue in chapter 9, the UK tax regime favours a couple where both earn less, rather than one partner earning a large amount and the other only a little.)

This contrast between working-class and middle-class fathers has been observed by social researchers for decades: "The married men in middle-class occupations expressed a desire to be more involved in the daily life of their children and the home, but their relationship to work necessarily precluded this. In contrast, the men in working-class occupations who less frequently voiced this wish for more involvement were paradoxically carrying out more routine child-care and housework tasks," wrote two sociologists in the early 80s.[17]

Any sea change in men and women's roles when it comes to childcare can, therefore, only really be led by those of us who have the choice to change our own situations. And we have the influence, time and motivation to press for change among our employers, political leaders and others with power. Change has to start with those who have the power to change their own way of doing things, and who can afford to do so. And that means us, folks.

I make no apologies, too, for taking aim at middle-class *couples* in particular, and how childcare roles and responsibilities are shared out between them. For separated parents, estranged couples and single parents, their childcare arrangements and responsibilities also often carry far less choice. While those situations are still often very unfair when it comes to childcare, the reasons behind the imbalance can be far more complex than among most cohabiting couples.

Meantime, anecdotally at least, childcare in same-sex couples tends to square up a lot more fairly than in heterosexual ones. And anyway, the new fatherhood myth is located squarely within comfortable hetero-coupledom, not in gay parenting – which of course carries with it its own growing trends and overexcited newspaper features. When journalists write about a growing trend of fathers taking a fairer share of the childcare, they almost always mean fathers who are still living with the mother of their children. So it is to those couples (and the journalists who write about and for them) that this book is primarily addressed.

After all, it is right here in comfortable couple land where I myself live. And it is right here that, despite our protestations to the contrary, systematic inequality and unfairness in the parental share of childcare and working life persists.

★   ★   ★

So, if I'm calling for a fairer deal among middle-class parents, what kind of fair deal am I talking about? Surely, not symmetry?

Should he wash exactly the same number of babygrows as she does? Over any given period, should she be pulling on exactly the same number of booties as him, wiping up the same number of pools of sick? Do we need a blackboard with a list of jobs on it, that partners tick off to ensure they're doing exactly equal every day, week in, week out?

Symmetry, surely, fosters a clocking-in/clocking-out, tick-list, checks-and-balances type of child rearing that none of us signed up to, and which takes away all the spontaneity, and fun, and laughter, and love of having a kid. Surely, we have to accept that men and women are just different, that they have different roles to play when it comes to the tasks of childcare. Dads do some childcare-related things that women don't do, so that offsets the childcare-related things that Mum does. It might not be symmetrical, but in terms of jobs done, it is equal.

This differentiated childcare role seems to be exactly how we organise our non-working lives. Men make up the feed bottles, and women do the feeding. Men take the kids to the park, play rough and tumble on the lounge floor, while mums are more likely to do the reading and counting. Dads build the cots and bunk beds, while mums buy the duvet covers, change the sheets and do the shopping. And if we're talking about equality, on some surveys men actually do more playing with their young children than women do.[18] Do catch up, ladies.

At weekends, mothers spend around twice as much time on food management and household upkeep as fathers. Meanwhile, fathers spend one hour a day at weekends on construction, repairs and gardening, compared with 30 minutes by mothers.[19]

The difficulty is that this splitting of jobs actually results in a pretty raw deal for the women us blokes are supposed to love. By not even examining the different roles men and women play in the raising of our children, the work women do often remains more or less in the shadows. Men don't consider whether they could do more, because we don't even know the half of what women do to raise our children.

Men get the nice stuff – the fun play, the trip to the playground, the bedtime tucking in – while mum is busy brushing dried-on shit off yesterday's sheets, or scooping out porridge and crumbs from creases in the high chair. Who would want to do that crap, when the sun is shining and there's a swing to be swung and a see to be sawed?

Or let's put it another way. When was the last time Mum took the kids to the park on a Saturday afternoon, so that Dad could catch up with a few jobs around the house? Jobs like changing the kiddies' sheets, putting an extra wash on, sewing on some labels, and preparing a week's worth of individual portions of mushed carrot and sweet potato for baby's lunches? It doesn't happen, and why doesn't it happen? Because those jobs aren't fun – or at least they're not fun if you have to do them again and again and again, with little sign of your partner doing their own share.

(After all, any kind of work can be soul destroying if it's repetitive and boring and we don't feel we're being sufficiently thanked or even acknowledged for what we're doing. It's just that with childcare, there's no corporate management structure to relieve the relentless toil or recognise and celebrate our achievements.)

Here's the point, and it's missed by women, and more than gladly overlooked by men: this is not an equal swap. These women, the ones we're supposed to love and respect, are being left with the shit jobs. Left by us, but also by our cultural expectations of women and men's roles when it comes to childcare. Now we can all put up with shit jobs for a while, but they're made ever crapper if we feel we've been left to do them alone, that they are our responsibility, just part of our life, and we have no choice but to do them.

In the main, the traditionally male bits of childcare aren't worth a fraction of the traditional women's bits of childcare, not in terms of toil, and frustration, and muck, and dissatisfaction.

Unlike a man who gets to choose what nice or nasty jobs to do – either because he literally does choose, or because culturally we are expected to do certain things and not expected to do others – the woman has no choice. She picks up what's left because if she doesn't do them, they won't get done. And when children are involved, things do simply have to get done: the woman is often the parent of last resort.

Meanwhile, men are regarded as heroes – and women considered lucky – if their men do take responsibility for some of the more traditional women's childcare roles, because at least they're doing something. Something is better than nothing; something is better than what her friends' husbands do, so let's not push him too hard, eh? If men do one or even two days of childcare each week, they're practically gods in their own eyes, and in those of every woman and grandma in the street. Granddad, meanwhile, thinks he's a pansy.

If Dad is doing something more than our own fathers did, then hey, we should be thankful. It doesn't matter that the jobs men receive a medal for, women just do and have been doing since men went out hunting mammoth and women stayed behind to clean the cave. And while we're at it, children working in sweatshops is cool because at least we're not sending them up the chimney any more.

It's like the big meal that Dad cooks on a Sunday, and presents with a smart whip of a tea-towel and a flourish: Look, everyone, look! Look what Daddy created! Who can blame the woman who has cooked every other meal this week from rolling her eyes as she washes up afterwards, which is fair, because after all, he did cook the meal.

By laughingly throwing off any striving for symmetry as some kind of regimented childcare communism, we actually allow a fundamental inequality to persist, however much the new father we claim to be. It allows men to assume they're doing their fair share because most don't acknowledge, or even know about, what their partners simply do every day, relentlessly, without hope of a break and without expecting a medal.

The truth is this: when it comes to babies and small children, there are two things and two things alone that women only can do: give birth and breastfeed.

That's it. That's the sum total of the inequality that nature has dealt us. The action of squeezing a baby out of your uterus and having a baby suckle directly from your nipple. They're two things that men simply cannot do. We can try, but in this instance I would admit defeat. It's not in our genes.

But after six months, maybe a year, when breastfeeding is done with, that's it. And if you are not breastfeeding – and nearly half of women aren't after six weeks – a fairer deal can come a whole lot earlier.[20] There is no natural, biological, spiritual or social reason why men and women can't do exactly the same tasks in relation to their children, at exactly the same frequency, and to exactly the same extent. There are no men's and women's jobs.

Of course symmetry is crazy and impractical and joyless and unrealistic. And of course life doesn't really work that way. As children grow up, changes happen, and we continually adjust to their and our own needs.

But surely it should be something for us at least to strive towards. By setting out, even metaphorically, a list of the multitude of tasks it requires to feed, wash, entertain, comfort, clear up after, maintain and educate a baby or toddler, at least both Mum and Dad can consider which jobs would make a decent swap. At least we could argue about it fairly.

It would allow every couple to look at each task and ask themselves, well actually, why couldn't that be Dad? Mum can say: what good reason have you got not to scrub the skids from our little boy's pants, because if you don't, guess who has to? Call it project management, if you like.

And, by the way, the best time to have this childcare call

to account is not when your kids are packed off to school for half the day or more. Childcare symmetry becomes a whole lot easier then. The hard slog of childrearing has already been done. Four or five years of hard slog. The nasty jobs have long become invisible by the time the school bell rings. Even the mum doesn't realise she's doing them.

The big secret about childcare tasks is that the majority of them get so much easier the more you get used to them. What seems impossible with a newborn in the first week or two becomes just a pain in the arse by week four, and second nature by the end of the second month.

And once you've developed your technique for getting out of the house with your travel system, or getting food into the baby's mouth, or the correct way to pre-soak clothes so the stains come out rather than hold their positions after a hot wash — well, it's all just too much effort, isn't it, to let another person learn from the beginning all over again, because they'll do it wrong anyway, and wouldn't it be quicker... oh, for Christ's sake, just let ME do it!

Equality should start before the baby is even born. Before Dad goes along — or chooses not to go along — to antenatal classes. Like using washable nappies, introducing equality from the beginning and not even allowing an alternative is far easier than starting at a later stage. If you feel your partner is doing their fair share, rather than leaving you to struggle alone, the whole baby experience suddenly becomes a whole heap more fun. Equality becomes a habit.

"How do you do it?" men who do more childcare tasks are often asked. "How do you let him do it?" the women in their lives get asked just as frequently. The truth is, it's easy if you've been doing it since day one. Easy because you don't know any other way.

4

'Doing babies'

SOMEWHERE BURIED FOUR levels deep on a hard drive containing our family's digital photo archive, tucked into a folder with an inconsequential title like "R – first months", is a set of photographs I took of my wife with her breasts out.

Far from titillating, these were photos I took at 2.45 in the morning. She's sitting up at the end of our bed, her face red and creased with tiredness, her messy hair piled on one side, stuck to her forehead and hanging over her eyes. Held to her over-sized left breast, wedged under her arm at what looks like an impossible and incredibly uncomfortable angle, is our son Reid.

I didn't get up in the middle of the night to take these pictures to mark the wonder of childrearing, or the simplicity and beauty of a nursing mother. I took them because we'd just spent nearly two hours trying to get our screaming son to take the breast, and after finally managing it, we wanted a picture we could try to imitate next time.

We'd tried every position and angle: lying down, sitting up, on the side, upside-down, "lie on the bed and simply let your warm hungry baby find you" as one – soon to be torn up – parenting book had advised. Rugby-ball position, traditional position, from the left, from the right. Jump up and down and to the knees. And somehow, for a brief few minutes, we'd got it.

There was no way I was letting this pass. This was evidence. A blueprint. Tomorrow morning I'd print out these photos, and they would be our instruction manual. They showed, to the millimetre, the exactly perfect position. The only position from which our son had decided he would feed.

My wife was so tired and grateful he had finally latched on, she didn't mind me – naked myself – snapping her from every angle. I could have been broadcasting it live over the internet, and she would still have sat there in zombie gratefulness as Reid relieved some of the pressure from her full-to-bursting boobs. She would, of course, kill me if I told anyone I still had the photos.

If getting Erin to take the breast was a challenge, persuading Reid to breastfeed was no less than a two-person job. In the middle of the night, in the middle of the day, in cafés, in the library, on a bench in the street, the routine was the same. The bugger just wouldn't open his mouth, and that meant a two-pronged attack. Sarah would hold him in just about the right position, holding the back of his head so his face sat just underneath the nipple. Because from that angle she couldn't see him, I'd kneel or stand over them both, with my hand resting on her arm. When he dared open his mouth to cry, or yawn, or breathe, for even one second, I'd push the whole package – baby, head, Sarah's arm and hand

– up, slightly across, and forward onto her chest, in one swift, desperate movement.

If Reid didn't immediately bite down, forcing Sarah to yank him away from her bleeding nipple, we'd wait, with me still crouching over the top of both of them, absolutely still. Completely silent, while we counted to ten. If we'd got it right, Reid's temples would start pulsating, telling us he was feeding (which happened very rarely). If we'd got it wrong he'd drop right off again and start howling madly for the nipple he'd just been offered as if we'd purposefully prised him away from it (which happened very frequently).

Did we argue about the best way to breastfeed him, the exactly correct position? You bet. Would we have tried anything to stop the crying and get him to feed? Absolutely ANYTHING. Did we eventually get there, and have him habitually and comfortably feeding from the breast at will? Yes... eventually. Months later, we would look back on those photos, smile and reminisce. About two months later. Was it really that bad? Yes, it bloody well was.

I make no judgement here on women and couples who decide breastfeeding is not for them, except that I don't bloody blame you. But Sarah and I decided from before Erin was born that we would, together, give breastfeeding everything we had got. We'd read the literature and were convinced that it was one of the best things we could do for our newborn. We made our choice, and no matter how hard it was at times, we were both too stubborn to give up – though we came close at times.

One thing that we'd decided even before Erin took her first tentative – and for Sarah extremely painful – gulps of breast milk on the Ulster Hospital labour ward was that breastfeeding, and all the stress, night-time wake-ups, mess and embarrassment that would come with it, would be a joint enterprise. If we were to raise our children as equally as possible, that meant starting with the toughest equal share of the lot: breastfeeding.

Breastfeeding can be the one of the earliest opportunities for men and women's role in childcare to become unfair. In fact, some argued we should formula feed our babies so as to remove this discrepancy. Sarah and I found ourselves having to think creatively about how to square the circle of being both committed to breastfeeding, but also committed to sharing the work.

Some 81% of UK women at least begin breastfeeding. At six weeks half of mothers are still breastfeeding, and a third at six months.[1] Simply on a physiological level, it is an activity that excludes men. It then strengthens the bond between woman and baby, separating the dad from the action. And often giving him a reason to excuse himself. What am I supposed to do, I don't have the... *equipment*?

The path to inequality in childcare that starts at breastfeeding quickly leads to a wider gulf and stronger excuses. If he's not feeding the baby in the night, well there's not really much point in his getting up in the night at all. What's the use of both parents being tired? A 2011 survey revealed that two in five fathers don't get up in the night to tend to their babies. And that logic quickly turns into a more ingrained separation. If he's not getting up in the night, there's not much point in his sleep being disturbed while she does. So, maybe he'll just kip in the spare room or on the sofa for a few nights. After all, he does have to go to work in the morning. (Apparently, she can catch up on sleep during the day.)

A third of fathers sleep apart from their partners to get a good night's sleep during the first year of their baby's life. One in ten moves out of the marital bedroom entirely.[2]

What started as an admittedly tricky physical challenge during the first few weeks of a newborn's life – men don't lactate – quickly turns into a lasting separation between father and baby, and a lasting inequality between Mum and Dad.

Baby becomes the woman's job, particularly at night. Getting a good night's sleep, then getting up in the morning to do a day's decent work for decent pay becomes a man's. What starts as convenience turns into habit, quickly becomes ingrained and then becomes just the way things are: women's roles and men's roles.

I often think one swift answer to this whole inequality might be for us all to recognise, officially and once and for all, that looking after a baby during the day *is a day's work*. It's a job. It's not some relaxed day off, a holiday from the tough grind at the office. Both are work, both are vital, both should be rewarded. And neither should automatically trump the other. And, of course, both can be done as a whole, or chopped up, swapped and shared, by parents whether they have a willy or not.

Many couples don't, of course, allow the difference between their roles to be wedged in so deep. The majority of fathers don't vacate the marital bed, and many, many men do get up in the night. But on a cultural level, there is the often unspoken justification that the physical differences between men and women are reason enough for women to do more of the childcare. And that attitude often begins at breastfeeding.

But let's rewind.

There is very strong evidence indeed that a man's active involvement in childcare from the very earliest hours, days and weeks of a baby's life are massively beneficial to his partner, to their child and to him. Skin-to-skin contact between men and their babies in the labour ward leads to caesarean-delivered babies being calmer and more likely to stop crying, and might be beneficial to all babies however they are delivered.[3] When men are involved in childcare right from the beginning, they are more likely to stay involved as the child grows up. Indeed, it starts even before the baby is born. Fathers who have participated in babycare courses take on more care of their babies than fathers who have not. Such fathers keep closer to their babies, engage in more face-to-face interaction with them, smile at, look at and talk to them more. [4] For breastfeeding in particular, the active involvement and encouragement of men leads to more couples persisting and succeeding with it, with all the health benefits that brings for our babies.

It turns out that getting up in the night to comfort and change baby, getting involved in breastfeeding or bottle feeding, playing with, cuddling and talking to our babies before they can focus their eyes, smile or do anything interesting at all, is one of the most important things that new dads can do.

Which makes the chuffed and self-satisfied claim of one father I know that "I don't DO babies" all the more exasperating. No, men don't have breasts. But like so many of the issues in this book, to throw our hands up and go and sleep in a different room shows a sorry lack of creativity about what couples could be doing to keep men involved.

In *Meet The Fockers*, one of the US blockbuster moves that made Ben Stiller a star, Robert De Niro plays a grandfather who is trying to engage fully in the life of his grandson. Aside from all the usual oh-so-funny drinking breast milk gags, one memorable scene has De Niro strap on a synthetic breast, through which his daughter's expressed milk will be fed to his grandson. (De Niro won an Oscar for his performance... in another film.)

For my wife and me, the solution wasn't anything quite so radical, nor was it made of rubber or plastic. It was simply a strategy that has held solidly for us in pretty much every aspect of childcare since Erin was born. It is the dangerous, radical, unusual and complicated strategy of... taking it in turns.

While Sarah owned the breasts from which our children would suckle, that didn't mean she had to be the one getting up in the night for the babies, changing their nappies, comforting them and putting them back to bed.

One day out of two, she did do all of these things. And then the next night when the baby cried it would be me that got up blurry eyed. I'd lift the baby from the cot, change the nappy and sodden babygrow and replace with new ones, and then I'd take the baby to my wife. And then, almost without waking her – but never quite managing it – I'd help the baby to latch on to her breast as she lay in bed. I learned, from the elastic band on my wife's wrist, which boob's turn it was to be suckled. Then, as my wife fell in and out of sleep while the baby happily gorged away, sometimes for 45 minutes, I'd sit by the bed watching them and trying to keep my eyes open.

I didn't always succeed, but if I did drop off it was considered very acceptable for my wife to elbow me in the ribs when the baby had finished. I'd then burp the baby, check the nappy again and carefully (gratefully) place them back in their cot to sleep. For another couple of hours. Until the whole thing would start again.

I make it sound simple, and of course it didn't start off that way. Getting the babies to feed in the first place took both of our wits and patience, and deprived both of us of sleep for some considerable and miserable weeks. But once we'd got into a comfortable routine it became, well, easy. OK, not easy. Nothing about babies is easy. But better. And fairer.

Of course in the later months of both my children's lives, my share of daytime childcare wouldn't have been possible at all without Sarah's willingness to attach a mechanical pump to her engorged bosom twice a day, to express milk for me to feed them while she was at work.

Expressing. That's a lark. Twice a day, without fail – on pain of both a starving baby and exploding boobs – Sarah had to sit for at least half an hour, with a machine whirr-click-sucking at her breasts. And that machine was in turn plugged into the mains.

After going through that, as well as all the bottle washing, sterilising and transporting all the equipment wherever she went, if I or the baby wasted so much as a drop, my life wasn't worth living. In those cases, it very much *was* worth crying over spilt milk.

Any bloke who thinks life is tough and annoying because they have to do the morning commute every day, or suffer IT problems from time to time, should have a crack at expressing milk day after day. It wasn't pretty to watch so I can't imagine what it was like to have to do it. Actually, I can imagine what it was like to have to do it.

Let's face it, most blokes whose partners have expressed milk have probably had a sly go on the expresser themselves (and maybe a sip of the stuff too?). I found my hairy torso meant the vacuum couldn't get any purchase, so I couldn't have extracted any milk even if I had wanted too. Or been capable of lactating. Anyway, it might have been fun once. But every day, twice a day, sometimes with an audience of friends over for dinner, for a whole year? No thanks.

I cleaned out our freezer recently and found two bags of frozen breast milk deeply embedded in a couple of years' ice

build-up. Waste not want not, I said, but Sarah wasn't sure
what her milk's use-by date was. But reminded of the daily
struggle expressing had been, we both breathed a sigh of
relief that we'd left that particular baby chore long behind.

I'm certainly not saying our one-night-on/one-night-off
routine, followed by expressing, is the only way to *do* fairness
when it comes to baby feeding. What I am suggesting is that
men and women can go a whole lot further between them
to explore what might work. They might take it in turns for
each feed. Or to offset the night breastfeed, the man might
willingly take on another time-consuming and boring core
job, like doing all the washing, hanging up and ironing every
single day until the baby is weaned. Or maybe they get the
kids up every morning. That's a pretty fair swap.

In this department, those couples who choose not to
breastfeed really do have a head start. There's no physical
reason for men's equal involvement not to start from the
very moment baby comes home, if not even on the labour
ward. What matters is that couples try equality from the
outset instead of giving up at the first hurdle. And if some
form of equality is established from the very earliest days
of a baby's life, and if we men get to see it's not so difficult
after all, then perhaps that will influence how we as couples
organise other aspects of childrearing as the baby gets older.

We're setting ourselves up for a fairer deal. By starting
early, we realise we *can* do this stuff, it isn't some secret
knack that only women have. And as we enjoy a fairer
relationship with our partners and a better relationship
with our newborns, we might even start to feel better
about ourselves.

If there's one thing I've learned about being an equal
dad, it's that I should be proud that I've broken the mould.
I'm not looking for applause or a medal, but I still feel good

inside. And I know my kids are less likely grow up with some deeply ingrained notion that only women look after children. Instead, they see that whatever your gender, men and women can pretty much do the same things.

Incredibly, despite it being the most high profile and most often cited aspect of babycare, one third of fathers don't change their baby's nappy. A third don't bath their baby.[5]

When it comes to the jobs entailed in baby rearing, there is one necessary truth that men cannot escape. If men "don't do babies" then it means the women have to do what men won't. The more babycare that men excuse themselves from, the more babycare women have to pick up by default. We forget that being knackered and frustrated and bored is part of the deal of childcare. What did we expect when decided to have one? The jobs still have to get done.

If men are unwilling to share some of the negative (as well as the positive) aspects of childcare, what we are essentially saying is that we'd prefer our wives to endure the bad and good without us. What kind of men, husbands and fathers does that make us?

★ ★ ★

Erin had just started pre-school and we were off on a Wednesday afternoon to a birthday party for one of her new friends. Children's birthday parties – big ones, with balloons, and paper plates, and cake, and fizzy drinks, and dozens upon dozens of other people's children – would soon become a regular fixture in my life. But this was my first one, and to be honest I was a little bit nervous.

Erin was holding my hand for dear life, she also a little embarrassed to be plunged head first into a strange room with so much colour, mess and noise; dressed among her new friends for the first time not in her sweet pre-school jersey, but in her best party frock.

"Oh, hello Erin," says one of the mums to my daughter, welcoming her with a big grin on her face. "Is Mummy working today?"

So that's how it's going to be, is it?

"Er, hellooo," I felt like squawking. "Hellooo, can you see me? I'm here. Me, over here. The one standing right in front of you. The one's whose face you would be looking at if only you would actually make eye contact with me."

I'm sure she thought it was a lovely way to welcome my daughter to the party. But to me she might as well have told me to gather up my penis, my testicles, my broad shoulders and my frankly unwanted Y chromosome, and get the fuck out of there.

To start with, it would have been nice if she had said hello to me as *well* as my daughter. But that's just good manners, so I'll let it slide. But what's this "is Mummy working" crap? It says: I wish you'd brought your mummy with you, instead of this... man. And it implies that I'm the stand-in, the substitute. It assumes that if neither of us were working, it would of course be my wife – one of the girls – bringing Erin to the party. The only possible reason a man would be bringing their child out during the day – alone! – would be that the mum couldn't make it. Otherwise, he'd be tagging along behind her, or more likely at home nailing two bits of wood together and drilling things in his shed.

The overarching problem with this seemingly innocent question is that it fails a simple test I've devised to measure whether someone gets what equal parenting is about. Would you say the same to my wife? Would you say to our daughter, failing to look at Sarah in the eye, "Is Daddy working today?" and then leave her to go and sit alone at the end of the table and not speak to her for the whole of the rest of the afternoon?

Honestly, women readers, how many times have you, while out during a week day with your children (or even on a weekend), been asked by a puzzled questioner where your partner is? Because I get asked it all the time. I get this kind of thing from women around town, in shops, in cafés, at bus stops, from people I don't even know.

"Oh, that's nice. Is your wife working/shopping/round the corner/letting you have a go/on a spa weekend/in police custody today?"

Sometimes I feel like replying: "Oh, no. She's just not here. Well, actually, I've killed her. I ate their mum yesterday. And all just so I could spend time with my little ones in town being smiled at patronisingly and being asked stupid questions. But, do have a nice day. Reid, darling, please do stop pouring milk all over the table." But that might give equal dads a bad name.

Here's some things women probably shouldn't say to men with babies:

"Ahh, you look like you've got your hands full."

"So, Mum has put you in charge today, has she?"

"Doesn't she need a coat? Don't you think she'll catch a cold dressed like that?"

"So, where's Mummy today?"

"Oh, my husband does loads too."

"Ah, is it Daddy Daycare today?"

"So it's break-the-rules day, yeah?"

"Have you lost your job?"

"Excuse me, no offence, but is this your baby?"

"Oh, it's not half-term, is it?"

"I bet you their mum does all the cooking and cleaning though…"

"I've been watching you for a while, and I'm very impressed. You're a very good dad."

To be honest, it's unfair to blame mums themselves. This unequal attitude is ingrained into our very psyche from the moment of our children's conception, if not before. From the marketing and welcome, to the language used when you get there, antenatal classes, baby and toddler groups, playgroups, pre-schools and primary schools assume and reinforce the idea that it is Mum doing the job of parenting.

At the open day for new parents, the teacher at my children's school said things like "And when Mummy picks the children up from school…" or "Mums often come in to me and say…". After Erin had started primary school, one woman parent said directly to me as I was picking up my daughter: "Yeah, it's difficult these hours, because the children come home tired at three o'clock and all the mums have still got to cook their dinner."

Reformed lad's mag journalist Martin Daubney writes about being asked to leave a playgroup with his baby boy because a woman there wanted to breastfeed. For him it was the last straw. He signed his child up to nursery as soon as possible, and got out of being a stay-at-home dad altogether (to which some women internet posters quite fairly commented: "lucky you – most mums don't get to throw in the towel, they just get on with it").

This is in no way scientific, but indicative none the less: in the week I was writing this section I took a notebook along to both our local library sing along and our local playgroup, to note down what happened. At the sing along, a busy and popular affair at Colchester library, there were 37 adults present, with an array of children. There were two men – me, and a chap who'd come with his wife. But he went straight upstairs to the adults' section as soon as the session started, leaving his wife and me, and our kids, to moo moo here and quack quack there without him.

At the playgroup, there were 25 adults present of which I was the only man. Though I tried to strike up conversation with a number of the women, only the organiser of the session (who, to be fair, actually looked a bit desperate for me to come again) and a granny would make conversation. At coffee time, I was one of the first to sit in the communal area with my drink. Every one of the women went and sat on the opposite side of the room, leaving me and my son to share our refreshments alone.

It wasn't, I'm sure, that the mums thought I was some kind of paedophile, using my son as an angle to their children. And it wasn't out of malice. It was probably that they didn't think we would have any shared experience to talk about, or any shared language to do it in. They assumed I didn't (like their own partners?) know much about babies, so they didn't make the effort to find out.

We're well into the 21st century; we've sequenced the human genome and placed a roving droid on Mars. Yet we're still filling our library and village hall notice boards with

posters advertising Mother and Toddler group, Mums and
Under Fives, and Pushy Mothers – all groups within reach
of my home in Essex. OK, our local library does put on a
Saturday morning session for blokes: *"R U Daddy Cool?
Come make some noise with your baby and toddler at our Daddy
Cool sessions."*

But honestly? R U crazy? What male of any age above,
say, seven would be persuaded to go to anything called *Daddy
Cool*, or *Who Let the Dads Out?* or even *Saturdads?* The thing
about male parents is that, for the most part, we're adults.
Why not talk to us and treat us that way?

Most of us don't want special dads-only groups, put on
every fourth Saturday but not when it clashes with the
football. So why not just make it really clear on posters and
leaflets that sessions are for both men and women, and you'd
be really pleased to see either or both of us there?

And when men do come to these things, please don't
act with shock or surprise, and definitely not horror. On
the flip side, don't treat us like we've just rid the Congo of
child soldiers either. Instead of thinking up wacky names
for your group to get us along, give us a welcoming smile,
include us in your language and eye contact when you're
talking, and encourage us to get involved alongside everyone
else. Because if you include us, ask us questions, encourage
us to be involved, the women there will take your cue and
include us too. And that means we might just come again.

There's nothing worse for a man at the school drop-
off, or at playgroup, than a clique of women who circle
the baby wagons and don't include any outsiders in their
familiar chat. To turn up to playgroup or the school gates
and have to stand on the outside of a tight little circle of
women is, to put it frankly, really unpleasant. And, sisters, it
does nothing to equal the playing field between men and

women either. What are you even talking about that is so interesting and important?

Another challenge is the assumed underlying sexualisation of contact between hands-on fathers and mums. I've never felt able to invite a woman and her child back to our house, so our kids can play together. I fear my approach might be taken as some kind of play for the mum herself, or at least that she would refuse because it might look a bit dodgy to her own partner.

As a full-time stay-at-home father who has experienced the same put it: "I can't walk up to a woman and introduce myself, it would feel like a come-on. But women do it all the time with each other. If a play date is proposed I would still give the mother's number to my wife for her to call and arrange it. I wouldn't make an arrangement to go round a woman's house if the husband was at work. You just can't get the sexual element out of it."

Men, of course, are hardly blameless in this separation at the school and playgroup gates. In fact, I have a theory about this whole men-in-group-childcare-setting thing. Men won't sit on the floor.

That's what it *all* stems from. And we definitely won't sit on those teeny-weeny chairs they have for the kids in pre-schools and playgroups. Look around you next time you're at a library sing along, a school meeting, a playgroup or a children's party. The women sit squeezed together onto the colourful rug on the floor or wedged onto those tiny plastic chairs. The men, if there at all, stand or sit on big chairs at the back. We don't *want* to be involved.

I'm at another child's birthday party, this time where a children's entertainer has been hired. There are a dozen singing and clapping children in a circle, throwing beanbags to each other, stamping their feet and bouncing up and down on a nice warm knee. And that, as usual, meant 11 pairs of nice warm women's knees, and mine. I was the only man who had joined the circle, singing and clapping along to the awful jingly jangly music.

It wasn't that there weren't any other blokes at the party. There were loads (this was a weekend event). But every one of them was standing round with his back to the wall, supping on a can of Foster's and watching as the women did the singing, and the rocking, and the silly games. And when the food came, it was the women – mums and grannies – who helped their kids get their crisps and teddy-bear sandwiches, their jelly and ice cream, and it was the women preventing their little ones from stuffing their fist into the birthday cake. (It was also the women washing up afterwards). Even the birthday boy's dad was standing at the back, as if this bit – the main event of the party for his child – had nothing to do with him.

Barbecues are the same, only with bigger chairs. Women play with and chase the toddlers around; men tend fire, crack open the tinnies and pour their wives the occasional glass of chardonnay. That's the rule; that's how barbecues go.

The truth is that I *do* really know what women are talking about in their tight little circles outside the school gates. They're talking about their children. They're sharing ideas, asking about progress at school, following up on illnesses, inviting each other on play dates. And these in-depth relationships all began – as friendships always do – with small talk. And if there's another thing we men don't like – in addition to our hatred of tiny chairs – it's small talk. So we exclude ourselves again.

But here's the big secret. Women don't like small talk either. They hate it just as much as us, but they use it at kiddies' groups because they need it to build solid networks around them. The relationships made at antenatal and NCT groups can last a lifetime. If men exclude themselves from the small talk, if we feel we're above it, we won't make it into the network. Then we feel excluded, so we excuse ourselves from taking our kids to groups altogether, and the whole cycle repeats itself.

There will always be cliques in any setting – work, rest or play – but the good thing about cliques is that there are always others left on the outside too. These men and women are fruit ripe for the picking: somewhere to start to build our own networks. And all it takes is to say "hello".

Now, I know this is difficult, and horrible, and boring for all of us, but here are a few other things you might say once that difficult first greeting has been uttered. Mums seem to have these things etched into their double X chromosome, so let me prompt the rest of us:

"Which one of these is yours?"

"Oh, he's lovely. How old is he?"

"I like his pushchair/jeans/shoes, where did you get them?"

"Is he sleeping through the night? How did that go?"

"How's his feeding/potty training/reading/ spelling going?"

"How's he getting on at school/swimming/ playgroup?"

"Does he have any brothers and sisters?"

It doesn't matter that you don't care about the answers to these questions. The person you're talking to doesn't give a crap about your answers either. Just nod along as if you are interested, because we all have to start somewhere. Before you know it you'll be sitting drinking coffee together like the best of mates, probably slagging off that clique of women and tut-tutting over the naughty boy who always seems to spoil everything for your oh-so-perfect children.

After all, don't most stag weekends start with small talk among a bunch of blokes who barely know each other? Twenty-four hours later we're hanging off each other's shoulders like blood brothers, telling each other we'd like to shag their mum.

Men have to act out the change we'd like to see; it won't be handed on a plate to us along with a chunk of sickly birthday cake and a few Hula Hoops. If men want better treatment at the school gates or kiddies' parties, we have to act in a way that will earn us a better reception. We have to roll our sleeves up and get stuck in, just like the mums have had to.

But there's another thing, and this is difficult to take: it's not about you. Playgroups and pre-schools and the library sing along are there in part to make parents feel comfortable and to help them feel less isolated. But they're also there for our children – so they can have a good time, learn and socialise. Surely, even if it's absolute hell for us, we should go if it benefits our own children? We can't scurry away because the mean girls won't talk to us, and the playgroup leader always says "mummy".

We have to do the small talk, and the floor sitting and the public nursery rhyme singing. We must go to these things even if they're uncomfortable for us, because they are of huge benefit to our children. But also, the more of us that get stuck in, the better reception we will receive, the more inclusive these places will become, and the more other men will join in too. Meanwhile, those initially suspicious women will gradually become friendlier, then even mates. The barriers will gradually break down. That's good for our kids, for us, and for families in general.

But, of course, it is incredibly difficult to act out that kind of change if blokes don't turn up to these things in the first place. And that's the biggest problem of all. We should take our kids to these places – but most men don't.

5

Choosing to do childcare

ONE OF THE more painful experiences for any father is when, during some game or other you're playing with your toddler, they pitch over and hurt themselves. First there's the unbelievably long period of *hurt or not?* silence, where the kid opens their mouth as if to cry but nothing comes out. And then the bawling begins. In earnest. Dad approaches to hug and reassure, only to be pushed away by his own child, who runs to Mum instead with their tears.

Ouch!

It's painful because your child has hurt themselves, and for most parents just that is like a little knife stab right there. None of us can bear to see our own children in pain. But that knife is twisted when it is their mum they run to for comfort, even when you're closer, ready with open arms, and desperate to make it all better.

I spent a difficult few hours at a barbecue once with loads of mums, dads and kiddies. In one family there, the little girl would not let her mother out of sight. Whenever Dad tried to pick her up, play with her, or even offer her food, she would screech and turn to her mum with arms outstretched. Whenever her mother wasn't in immediate eye line, the toddler would call out one of the only words she could say – *mummy, mummy, mummy* – over and over again.

If it was annoying for the rest of the guests, it must have been heartbreaking for the father to be rendered so obviously unwanted and unneeded, especially in front of his friends. However much he laughed it off in a 'what can you do, kids eh?' way, the deep hurt was etched on his features. There are few things more embarrassing in front of other people when you're trying to show what a good dad you are than for your own child to say to you: I want Mummy, not you!

Our traditional set-up of mum as primary childcarer tends to exacerbate the emotional distance between men and their children. And that's not good for women, or our children, and it's not good for men either. Much is made of Dad taking over the kids on the weekend to give Mum a break after her week of childcare. What really tends to happen is that Dad deals with the weekend playing and fun, the buying of ice creams and the swinging of swings. But when things get hairy – the scraped knees, the refusal to buy a toy, the tantrums – Mum gets dragged in to deal with the fallout.

It's often I'll hear a child cry: "I want Mummy to change the nappy." And what more prompting does a man need to hand the job over? Hardly the break she was promised, but one created by the stronger emotional bond she's had the time to build with her children. Dad feels further alienated and excluded, left to feel he's playing a complementary part at best. A glorified babysitter, not a fully involved and valued parent.

I've already written about what a pain in the arse child-care can be: how childcare days can be boring, frustrating, depressing and desperate, and that's one of the reasons why men are so reluctant to do it. But by excluding themselves from baby and childcare, men are also comprehensively missing out on the best bits about children and childcare too. By rejecting the rough, they're missing out on the smooth. And it's the smooth that makes everything worth it in the end; even the hardest parts of childcare become easily bearable.

Just as it hurts when your little one runs to Mum for comfort, men are hurting themselves and their relationship with their babies by not taking the opportunity to have amazing experiences with their children while they're still very young. They're missing that satisfaction men can feel that starts when they really *can* tell the difference between their baby's hungry cry, their tired cry and their wet cry. A natural bond and affinity with your little one that just gets stronger from there.

When I started caring for Erin one day a week, the first thing that struck me was the absolute mind-numbing boredom of it all. She didn't do much to entertain me; she could barely smile and spent half her time asleep. The rest, she was crying and whining. Just what the hell was I supposed to do all day?

In those early weeks, I think we were both desperately waiting for Sarah by the end of the day, if only to break the monotony. Erin, it turned out, was as bored as I was. Once I'd realised this, it was like a light going on. The day I made it a rule that Erin and I would never sit in our flat all day, it became a whole lot easier. Whatever the mess inside and whatever the crappy weather outside, we would venture into the world to seek some fun. Even if that just meant a very long, leisurely shop in Tesco, with lunch in the cruddy café afterwards.

Here's what women don't tell men about childcare. Along with the grubby and grotty bits that everyone complains about, there's nothing like being a free agent with your baby during the working day. And doing just what the hell you like. Whisper it, but that kind of day offers a sense of satisfaction, freedom and happiness that sitting at our desks at work could never deliver.

For a start, while Erin was busy becoming a connoisseur of her mother's breast milk, an expressed bottle of which I made sure was never more than a grab away, I developed in those days an honest-to-goodness addiction to very good quality coffee and cake. There was a time before kids when I could have told you the location, atmosphere and quality of beer sold at just about every public house in central London. Oh, how I miss those times. These days I can tell you where around Essex serves the best coffee, the most reasonably priced but delicious flapjacks and shortbread. I can point out the cafés where kids are made welcome, with a basket of toys below the counter. And, conversely, the cafés that don't go out of their way to cater for kids, and as such are absolute heaven if you want to sneak your toddler in for a quiet, unfussy sandwich.

Most mothers already know what I now know: it is one of the simplest pleasures in life to sit your baby on your knee, dropping crumbs into their hair as you both gorge on a heavily buttered tea cake. There's little better than a searingly hot Americano consumed while you and your child both – in respective ways – pore and pour milk over a newspaper. How wonderful it is to share a carrot cake with your kids, delicately dividing a slice into three and doling it out to amazed, wide-eyed gannets knowing they're about to enjoy it just as much as you are. How satisfying to see their cheeks so full of a cheese toastie they can barely breathe, let alone speak. And how satisfying to explain to a café owner the simple recipe for making a babycino, and to see pound signs ring up in their eyes as they calculate the massive profit margin of charging a quid for a bit of frothed-up milk and a sprinkling of chocolate powder.

Be warned, though, from someone who has developed more than a passing acquaintance with kids and coffee shops. Those big chains – the Costas and Starbucks and Neros – may be convenient, ubiquitous and reliable, but they have a very real problem with their toilets. As they should, those chains tend to have accessible disability-friendly loos, with all the adaptations that come with them: red emergency pull strings, low sinks and extra-large door handles. They only become a problem when, after you've taken your kids to the toilet, you decide to maybe sneak a quick poo yourself. That coffee can be pretty strong, after all.

There's only one thing worse than your toddler discovering how easy those big door handles are to turn while you're still sitting on the loo. It's when, at the same time, your other toddler discovers that the lovely red string with a triangle on the end makes a loud beeping noise when pulled, drawing the attention of every customer and staff member to you sitting there with your trousers down, with the door wide open, and your kids making a break for the high street.

The other joy of spending time in coffee shops, restaurants and other public spaces with your kids is you get to people watch with amusement. Specifically, you get to observe how absolutely terrible some mothers – yes, mothers – seem to be with their offspring. If ever argument was needed against the old idea that mothers are naturally better at childcare than men, just a short while observing from afar in a supermarket or in a park will quickly convince you.

There's one woman I particularly liked to watch at the library whose idea of allowing her toddler to enjoy themselves was to strap a set of those child reins onto them, and then let them roam in one big circle like a tethered dog, with her sitting at the centre holding the end and texting her friends. Then there was the time another mum dropped her kid off to play in the Early Learning Centre while she went off clothes shopping, leading to the staff wondering if they should call the police. If ever I was feeling inadequate or unsure of my parenting skills, a quick trip to town was all I needed to convince myself that I could be a whole heap worse.

The other thing about knocking around town on your own with your kids is that you, and you alone, get to make the decisions. Want to pop into the sci-fi comic shop? Great, your kids will love playing with the Ewoks. Want to pop into Superdry and not be harangued about spending £35 on a T-shirt? Go ahead, your little ones will be entranced by the bright colours. Want to get a cheeseburger and chips for lunch? Go ahead and take as long as you like – just remember to share. Hey, you know what? You can even take your baby into a pub and enjoy a pint and a packet of salt and vinegar on a weekday afternoon, while they have a snooze in their pushchair.

But the very best times are when you're with your kids and you see something in a shop you know they'll just love. I once saw the cutest set of tiny pink chequered pyjamas in a posh department store, while I was looking for some new socks. (Yes, I clothes shop for myself too; what a new man I am.) The pyjamas were expensive – probably because they *didn't* have Peppa Pig or Fifi on them – but do you know what? I bought them. I bought them because I wanted Erin to have them. I bought them because I could. I bought them because I'm Dad and I was in charge. I bought them because I knew how cute she'd look in them.

And in a strange way I was proud of myself for seeing something we both liked, and making the decision to get them without any reference to my wife. And I knew that Sarah would love them, for exactly the same reason. Those pink pyjamas were too big for Erin, then they fit just right, then they were a bit tight, then too small. Then my little boy Reid inherited them, and he looked just as cute as she did. Then he eventually grew out of them too. And then, with some friends visiting with their own baby girl, we passed the pyjamas on, and their little girl looked cute in them all over again. Is it weird to feel proud and fulfilled, in an entirely innocent, non-dodgy way, by a set of pink children's night garments?

Well I was proud, and perhaps men sometimes feel too embarrassed to go all gooey like that about the simple pleasures of parenting. It was a tiny and irrelevant thing to do, and something that women do most times they go out shopping. But for me those pink pyjamas made me feel like I was *doing* being a dad properly; a simple and sentimental testament (to me at least) to my being a good, thoughtful father.

Isn't it worth brushing up on our baby skills and putting in the babycare hours just for that? Or perhaps you would rather be at work looking at spreadsheets? No wonder all the evidence points to involved and part-time working fathers being happier and more satisfied with their family life.[1]

And there's something else about being a bloke with a pre-school age child and connecting with women out there with their kids too. I can often tell by their tone of voice when we talk about our respective children, or from their looks from across a café or a park, that they're... what is it.... challenged?

"Oh, my husband is really hands on too," said one woman struggling with two babies in a café. "He helps with bottle feeding and everything." Are these women being prompted to re-evaluate their own (and their partners') assumptions about who can and should be doing what? Are they thinking: "if he can do it, why can't we"? Clearly, they must have missed the whole doing a poo on the cafe floor incident, my mislaying of Erin in Poundland, the day I left Reid in his pushchair behind a reversing car at the swimming baths and countless other examples of my not quite top-notch parenting skills.

And if involved fathers have this effect on mothers out there on the high street, might we also have this effect on other fathers by being there, publicly doing and muddling along relatively competently doing childcare?

We don't like to admit it, but we like it when other people are envious of us. It shouldn't make me feel this way – because I'm only doing what mothers do pretty much every day – but I can admit to having felt a slight blush of pride as I have deftly and expertly fed my children in public, or dealt with their crying, or taken them off to the loo at just the right time. It has made me feel good to have women watch as I go about my business, perhaps to have influenced a few men to maybe go home that day and start to do a little bit more themselves.

I admit to more than a little smugness, but surely no more than the next bloke who has just brought home the new client everyone was after, or completed that roofing job ahead of time, or doubled his company's profit from that share deal and earned a tasty annual bonus into the bargain.

But the most amazing thing about spending more time with your children, particularly when they are very young, is that kids can be lovely. They are funny, and sweet, and gorgeous, and heartwarming, and adorable. They make you laugh, they make you smile, they make a lump form in your throat and a tear run down your cheek. And all just by being themselves. And they adore you. They really do absolutely and unconditionally love you to bits. They value your time, your attention, your chatter and your play more than anything else on earth. And the more you give them, the more they give back.

We pay good money to go and see movies or shows that make us feel good inside, that make us laugh, that make us cry. All of that is available in spades in our kids right now, and for free. For evidence of how obliviously happy and moved being with children can sometimes make us all – even to the point of a complete lack of awareness of how deathly boring our love for them is to other people – just take a look at some parent's endless Facebook posts about their amazing kids, and how special it is when they eat their dinner, or wear a hat at a jaunty angle, or colour in a picture, or say something silly, or fart in public.

Our time to achieve this kind of all-consuming emotional bond with our kids is limited. If we don't take the opportunity while we can, we may miss it forever. And while we're at it, we might be more likely to miss things like their first crawl, their first steps, their first mouthful of solid food, and even the first time they say Daddy. Nearly one in five fathers have missed four or more significant events in their child's life due to work.[2]

There are few men who aren't just a little bit jealous of the stronger relationship our children seem to have with their mums. We shouldn't have to be jealous, because those stronger bonds are available to men too. But they come with work. We have to develop them for ourselves. And that takes our time, which we must give unconditionally, sometimes sacrificially. Men aren't babysitters, standing in until Mum comes back. We are parents, and have a right to enjoy ourselves with all the creativity, moments of abandon and moments of inspiration that come with it.

Despite the grubbiness and the boredom and the dissatisfaction that doing a heavier portion of the childcare can sometimes bring, more men should just choose to have a crack at it and see how they get on. We should let our hair down a bit. You never know – particularly when our child brings their scraped knee to us for a rub and a kiss – we may just get to like it.

★ ★ ★

Choice is a word that is often bandied about when it comes to children and childcare. The state should keep its nose out and leave parents to choose what is best for their children. Parents should be able to choose whether the man or the woman does the majority of the childcare or the majority of the earning. Parents should be able to choose whether to stay at home with the kids, or send them to a nursery, according to their values and convenience.

I think this idea of choice trumping all shouldn't go without challenge, not least because all of us subconsciously make choices about our children and their care that we don't even realise we're making. We're all heavily influenced by social expectations, even if we don't notice it. What we sometimes call choice really is nothing of the sort. When a man automatically goes back to work after two weeks' paternity leave, because that's just what blokes do, is that a conscious choice to be the breadwinner or just something that kinda happened?

When we automatically send our kids to nursery because we want to go back to work ourselves, have we carefully considered our options and consciously chosen to do it? Or is it just something we'd assumed we'd do all along, without much thought? (That was certainly the case when we put Erin in nursery before she could even walk.)

When a woman claims to want to stay at home all day with the children, is that a freely made conscious choice or just the best option – given the pay gap, employer's expectations, social norms, and her own parental and societal conditioning – that she has to choose from?

I'm certainly not saying that choosing to be at home with the kids isn't a perfectly valid choice. Some women do consciously and freely make this choice. It's what they want to do, and all power to them. But surely it is just a little strange how few men seem to freely make that same choice for themselves? Couldn't social expectations be playing just as large a role as the choice we think we have?

Whatever we do, we tend to look back from where we've ended up and regard it as the result of decisions we've made. Then we declare our happiness with these choices, even though we often didn't consciously make them.

How many of us do actually discuss, weigh up, and really, knowingly make choices when it comes to childcare roles and responsibilities? And how many of us simply go with the flow, suddenly finding the choices we've unconsciously made have become set in stone, so we better be happy with them? This relentless tide that we're all carried along on, particularly in the bleary-eyed tiredness and the fog of ignorance when our children are first born, could be a key reason why childcare arrangements often turn out so unfair.

Men and women don't consciously choose to create inequality: men don't choose to be the breadwinner; women don't choose to sacrifice their careers. It just sort of happens because life ticks along and it's far easier to let it happen than to fight it when we're tired, and frustrated, and challenged. Perhaps if we'd known it was going to turn out this way, maybe we would have chosen differently. But by then, it's too late and too hard to reverse. By not actively choosing to be equal or fair in our childcare, we're accidentally choosing not to be.

Francine Deutsch, academic and author of US equal parenting manual *Halving It All*, argues that equal or fairer parenting has to be an active choice.[3] There's nothing automatic about sharing; it won't just happen by accident. Fairness takes effort and perseverance, because the barriers in the way of it are so strong. The moment we let things drift, we're swept along and suddenly find ourselves in an unfair situation. Equality is a constant process, not a decision made once that will endure without continuous effort.

6

Who's the daddy?

FINALLY, I THOUGHT, an article about someone like me in a national newspaper. This, I must read. It was not long after Erin's birth, in *The Guardian* family section of course. An article by a chap promoting his new book about 'how I learned to be a father', a memoir rather than a 'how to' book, about finding and forging a strong relationship with his young daughter.

The article centred around the author's first nights looking after his daughter, his wife having gone away on a hen weekend. And it featured funny and heartwarming anecdotes about his fumbling and finding his way through, his general buffoonery around his child.

The 'what is a man supposed to do with this crying, crapping thing?' gag was well worn even before the 80s film *Three Men and a Baby* (the one starring Magnum, Sam from *Cheers* and that guy from *Police Academy*). Now that it was certainly a story that was becoming familiar to me, I laughed

along heartily. But then I read on. It turned out this author
– the one being championed by the paper as one of a breed
of new, actively involved fathers – was writing about events
that happened at 16 months into his daughter's life, with his
wife "promoting me to sole parent".

His first time alone overnight with his daughter – his
'what am I supposed to be doing?' moment – came when she
was already a year-and-a-half old. Mum had, of course, left
a weekend's worth of neatly labelled dinners in the fridge,
and neatly folded children's clothes upstairs.

Is this really how low we have set the bar for our role-
model dads? Our celebrated example of an involved father
is merely someone who is capable and trusted by his wife
to look after their baby when she's already a toddler, when
she can just about walk, talk and feed all by herself?

If equal and involved fathers are looking for role models,
the bookshelves certainly don't seem to be the place to
start. There are, of course, a rash of baby books aimed
at fathers. They fall into two camps. First is the jokey
Aren't I a Useless Daddy gift books that treat kiddy-raising
like one big fart joke or an episode of *The Simpsons: The
Baby Owners Workshop Manual,* all designed and written
up as a Haynes car manual; *Commando Dad: Basic training*
("Take pride in your unit... Be prepared. Act in a way
befitting your Commando Dad status"); *The Bloke's 100 Top
Tips for Surviving Pregnancy* full of analogies about football,
fast cars and sheds; *From Lad to Dad: The ultimate guide to
pregnancy for blokes* with its full 200 words dedicated to
considering being a stay-at-home dad, entitled "Richard,
Judy and you?"

In the other, more earnest camp are books that tend to
have a few pages, perhaps a whole section on reducing your
working hours, but otherwise often reinforce the idea that

it will be Mum doing the majority of the work. With only two notable exceptions, Dad's role in these books is still to get home from work as early as possible, and help Mum with the night feeds from time to time.[1] The discussion frames men changing their work as an optional extra, whereas for women it is simply assumed.

For all the telling us how to do it that these books indulge in, no mainstream father's book I've read – and I've read a lot – features the idea that a dad might try to pursue equality in childcare. In fact, inequality is sometimes even reinforced in these manuals. Meanwhile, the one thing every fathers' book does seem to share in common is their obsession with how quickly, or otherwise, the bloke can get back to getting jiggy with his wife.

And it's not much use looking to the women's parenting books either, though all fathers have of course trawled through innumerable pregnancy and baby guides, despite their soft-focus pictures of women and their babies on the pastel-coloured cover. *The Gentle First Year* opens with an inspiring quote from "ancient Indian wisdom", which pretty much sets the tone for the rest of the book: "At every birth, two people are born – a baby and a mother."

Our own most-leafed pregnancy manual, *The Baby Book: How to enjoy year one*, endorsed by actress Gwyneth Paltrow no less, puts men firmly in their place: "Fathers can be invaluable in supporting and caring for both mother and baby in the early days at home. You will be much better able to rest if your partner can make you tea or breakfast in bed."

You might assume *The Natural Guide to Bringing Up Your Baby*, with its recycled paper, chapters on homeopathy and other natural remedies, and pretty right-on title, would be rather progressive on these things. Yet it contains not one single picture of a man in the whole photo-led book, and men or fathers feature nowhere in the index (though 'sleep – mother's lack of' does).

The Rough Guide to Pregnancy and Birth ("the soundest, sanest, wittiest advice you'll ever get") dedicates a generous half-page to "stuff for blokes", advising dads to just read the women's books since "it's all the same problems and the same advice". The author helpfully advises the expectant mum to share *her* birthing plan with the dad, so he knows what *she wants* when the time comes.

The problem with all of these parenting 'how to' books, and a lot of the men's fathering memoirs too, is that they tell the fatherhood story as it has been for time immemorial. This is how to make your way, given that women are best at and know more about childcare, and that blokes are generally bungling idiots around children (and prefer football and sheds and boobs); the best role a good father can play is to lovingly support women as they get on with it. There's little that urges men to take a proactive role and get good at this stuff for themselves. There's nothing that challenges women to take a back seat from time to time, and just let *us* get on with it and work out *our* own way.

Parenting books matter. It's an industry worth millions a year to publishers. Around a million pregnancy and parenting books have been sold in the UK every year, for the last five years, according to Nielsen BookScan. That's a quarter of a million more books than actual children born. And we all devour these books, learn from them and try to follow their advice – at least until we've realised it's all crap, and we do in the end find our own best ways by ourselves. Yet there are next to no books telling men directly that they should play a fair, active or even equal role, and certainly no memoirs telling us how to go about it. (I modestly hope this book goes some way towards filling the gap.)

Role models are important. Role models and their stories not only show us how, but also affirm the choices that we've made. If we see or read about someone else who is just like us doing something we might do, then we're more likely to follow suit. It's why life insurance adverts are full of finger-wagging just-past-middle-age grumps, and furniture adverts are packed with delirious young families falling into each other's arms in delight onto their brand new leather sofas. We see ourselves, and so we reach for our wallets.

We may not like to admit it, but all men are desperate to be kitchen geniuses thanks to the rise and rise of male celebrity chefs. But we'd also quite like a bash at living in the bush, killing and cooking squirrels, thanks to Bear Grylls and Ray Mears. Even Monty Don has made the digging of a hole and the good trimming of a hedge something blokes want to get good at. Role models offer a glimpse of the possible, while making their attempted imitation socially acceptable. So is it any wonder we men don't even aspire to equal parenting, let alone have the knowledge and tools to make it happen? We have no involved-father role models.

Now involved mothers, they're all around us. Mothers are conspicuous in their motherhood. The female boardroom manager successfully juggling high-end city life with tucking the kids in bed each night. The women TV presenters brandishing their engorging bellies week after week, to return a month later with baby in arms to tell enraptured audiences about the wonder of childbirth.

When you're home alone with your children during the week, you tend to listen to the radio a lot. I can remember in particular three separate radio interviews with women celebrities: TV presenter and one-time pop star Myleene Klass, Sharleen Spiteri from the band Texas, and indie front-woman Cerys Matthews. Each of the interviews centred on how they balanced their celebrity career with their children, and each had brought their child into the studio. The toddlers, in turn, gurgled and whinnied and made grabs for the microphone, all of course to the presenter's delight.

Remember my equal parenting rule? Have you ever heard a male celebrity interviewed at length about his children, or how he balances his tough recording schedule with nappy changes and feeding times? Has any radio programme you've ever heard featured a male rock singer in the studio with his two-year-old bouncing on his lap, interrupting the interview with a not so discreet fart? If I ever get interviewed about this book, I'm putting my lot up to the mic on general principle.

Women celebrities get asked in the media about their children, and the changes in their life that having them has brought. Male celebrities, at most, get asked if they made it to the birth, you know, what with recording the new album, touring and everything.

And that's just fathers who *happen* to be celebrities or public figures. Celebrity fathers are a whole different breed altogether. Could they be the new father role models I'm looking for? Brad Pitt. David Beckham. Jamie Oliver. These are our conspicuous celebrity dads, men who have made – by choice or by media – their fatherhood a key part of their public persona. Like it or not, they are the men we look up to for an indication about what fathers are *supposed to do*. Gary Barlow was crowned Premier Inn's Celebrity Dad of the Year in 2012, beating Peter Andre to the 'coveted title'. Rapper Jay-Z and footballer Cristiano Ronaldo were also in the running.

Now, I don't know much about these people or what great dads they may or may not be. But aren't we here mistaking being a great dad with simply being a well-known one?

Despite Premier Inn's claim that the award recognises "the celebrity dad who has impressed the nation by balancing a hectic public life with the demands of parenting", I've never heard anything of Brad Pitt turning down a film because he really ought to spend more time with his kids, or Peter Andre self-sacrificingly asking the media for privacy to protect his little ones.

John Terry won the Daddy of the Year Award in 2009 (run by Daddies Sauce); he wasn't at his twins' birth because his work – football – meant he was in Portugal, and he couldn't get back in time. By the way, that same year married Dad of the Year Terry began his infamous alleged affair with a team-mate's ex-girlfriend – something which cost him his England captaincy, but not it seems his Daddies' Sauce award.

Do we ever hear from celebrity dads what being a dad for them actual entails, what sacrifices and choices they've made for their children? Do male celebrities announce they're spending a few years away from the public gaze because they're going to be busy raising their newborn, like women celebrities sometimes do? Just having children for celebrity men seems to be enough to earn the accolade of Super Dad. Maybe Jamie Oliver does do the ironing and change the bed sheets, as well as most of the cooking, but unlike from women celebrities, we don't hear about it.

I actually think celebrity fathers are great. I'm a big fan of David Beckham and Jamie Oliver in particular. They both make fatherhood more visible, and they publicly and unashamedly show love openly for their kids. They make fatherhood seem a less *gay* thing for men to do. In turn, that makes it more acceptable for mere mortals like us guys to do the same. But as for challenging the stereotypes and showing that active fatherhood is more than being seen to kiss and hug your children in public, I'm not sure they quite do the job.

I want a drum beater, a dad who hollers from the rooftops that, as well as being a celeb, he's an out-and-proud involved parent. I want someone who encourages broadcast interviewers to ask him about feeding and sleeping regimes, about breastfeeding and expressing, about how the little one is getting on at nursery, and the challenge of finishing a photo shoot in time to make the school run. That's if the presenter can get a word in over the gurgling from the newborn he's brought into the studio.

In films, male parents get a similarly rough ride – by which I mean the subject is overemphasised or they're invisible. That a man is looking after a child *at all* is sufficient plot for any number of mad-cap movie capers like *Mr Mom, Mr Nanny, Daddy Daycare, Big Daddy* and, of course, *Kindergarten Cop*, which – ha ha ha! – placed Arnold Schwarzenegger as a primary school teacher (only, shhh!, he was really a police detective).

The exception is films where the man's active fatherhood is brought on abruptly, undesirably and tragically, but ends with a tear-jerking, life-affirming resolution. In other words, the mum dies or abruptly leaves. Films like the award-winning *Genova*, featuring Colin Firth, Will Smith's *The Pursuit of Happyness*, or *Jersey Girl* with Ben Affleck. Films of such unusual tragedy and striving against the odds are, of course, perfect film-awards material. But there are few films where a man actively involved in fatherhood is not *the* plot itself, the very reason for a film's existence. Meanwhile pretty much every appearance in a film of a woman looking after children goes by without any comment, or poignancy, whatsoever. A film about a woman bringing up her child after the tragic death of her husband just wouldn't be made, and it certainly wouldn't win any awards. Motherhood is just what women do. What's so special about that?

TV is the same. No regular UK soap or drama features an active, involved father except where they have been forced into it by a tragedy and have become *single* fathers, which is a whole separate issue. No male character looks after the children because, say, he and the mother did the sums, and read the research, and thought, well, maybe this is the fairest and best way for our little ones. The closest came in *Coronation Street* in autumn 2012, when Tyrone became a stay-at-home dad. But that was against his will, and only because he was afraid he would lose contact with his daughter Ruby if he didn't.

I'm being wilfully naïve, of course. Soaps and drama tell exceptional stories – that's why we watch them. Active fatherhood is going to be done as a big issue if it is going to be covered at all. Just as surely as one square in east London will unfathomably experience dozens of murders over a decade. But apart from following a tragedy or some blackmail plot like in *Coronation Street*, I'm still waiting for the active fatherhood storyline to be covered at all.

If you're a fan of Scandinavian drama – as many of us have recently become – then you will be familiar with a foreign exception. The first series of *Borgen*, a political drama set in the Danish parliament, saw a woman become prime minister, leaving her husband – the guy who shot Sarah Lund at the end of season two of *The Killing* – expected to be the perfect house-husband. It is he who has to bring up the children pretty much alone, and to have dinner on the table in time for his wife to not come home and eat it.

The upside-down 'women satisfies ambition while dad stays at home' plot gave the whole issue of men's roles, ambition, men versus women parental relationships, and men's relationships with their children, a thorough airing that UK domestic drama and soap has so far conspired to avoid. As well as decent watching, *Borgen* made for great social comment. Even if – spoiler alert! – the whole new father experiment eventually collapsed, with the put-upon husband having an affair, divorcing the prime minister, and rupturing their once happy and secure family life. Essentially, he couldn't take the role reversal. (Or to put it another way, *Borgen* wouldn't have made anywhere near as good a drama if the prime minister had been a man, and his long-suffering wife had been left at home with the kids. That's not even a story, it's just normal.)

So no role model there – or no *decent* role model at least – even in the often-cited progressive-parenting nirvana that is Scandinavia.

I know there is an apparent contradiction here. I'm calling for higher-profile examples of active and involved fathers in popular culture, but also for fathers who do a fairer share not to be regarded as exceptional heroes (on a good day), or freaks and worse (on a bad). I do want *Coronation Street* to make a storyline out of a family deciding the father will play an active role in childrearing, just as *Borgen* did. And I do want a public debate about all the difficult contradictions, challenges and failures that story stimulates. But I also want there to be fathers on soaps, in films, in politics and public life, who look after children and that's just what they do, there's no big deal. The root of this contradiction is that the new fatherhood myth tells us that active and involved fatherhood is already happening and already normal. And that's just not the case.

It *is* still unusual for men to be seen with babies, and active fatherhood does still make for a great media storyline. It remains a big issue that needs to be fully explored on TV. *Borgen* aside, we have so far missed the 'dealing with the issues' bit. Gay relationships were once a big storyline

on soaps; now rightly they're merely part of the character
background against which other plots roll out. Active
fatherhood needs to go through the *look at the freak* stage, to
come out the other end and become normal, unremarkable
and everyday. When 'father looks after baby' is no longer
a story, new fatherhood will no longer be myth. So let's
all just get the freak show over and done with as soon
as possible.

* * *

While we're on *Borgen*, maybe we should look to our own
political leaders for an indication of what active fatherhood
is all about. After all, the most high-profile men in British
politics at the time of writing are prime minister David
Cameron and deputy PM Nick Clegg. Both were conspicuously highlighted at the time of their election as fathers
with young children. They were, if the coverage was to be
believed, determined to usher in a new style of doing politics
that didn't exclude their domestic roles and responsibilities.
It was as if in 2010 we had – almost by accident – gone and
elected a pair of *bona fide* new fathers.

In those heady early days, at a time when the new fatherhood myth was particularly rampant, Clegg and Cameron
jostled to out-dad each other. As the coalition government
was finding its feet, newspapers were told that Cameron and
Clegg had been bonding over the construction of an IKEA
cupboard for Cameron's new baby at Downing Street.[2]

In 2008, even before his election as prime minister,
Cameron invited the cameras into his home to film his
family life – in stark contrast to Gordon Brown's fierce
protection of his family's privacy.

"To me, nothing informs my thinking more than family

because I think it's the most important thing there is in our society," Cameron said in defence of letting the cameras in. His 'Webcameron' films painted the PM-in-waiting as a hard-working, child-juggling, down-to-earth bloke of the people, cooking tea while his children ran around his feet and the family's washing hung in the background.

Soon after the May 2010 election, Cameron won much political ground by ostentatiously brandishing his second child, Florence, born in August of that year. Meanwhile, his wife Samantha was giving interviews to magazines emphasising how Dave was a fantastic dad and great cook, and that they had a very equal relationship. Much was made by the media of Cameron taking paternity leave after Florence's birth.

In the early days of the new government, Cameron was more than happy to be pictured with his kids, on the school run and taking them to the football. In 2011, he allowed *The Sunday Times* to follow him for a week, with the resultant sympathetic images – including one with him strapped into a BabyBjörn, talking on his mobile – doing his involved-new-father image no damage at all.

One academic has gone so far as to suggest this persona was created specifically to contrast with Cameron's policies to shame absent fathers, something he made a big issue of during 2011 following widespread rioting among teenagers across the UK.[3] Kissing babies is nothing new for politicians, but here was one – with the help of his PR team – actively and carefully constructing an involved fatherhood image. Just like Tony Blair – the first prime minister to have a baby while in office – did before him. No mention was made of David Cameron's full-time nanny. She didn't appear on Webcameron either. In fact, the nanny only came into public view during a media storm about her visa.

Nick Clegg too became a father again during the earliest days of the coalition. In 2011 he told the *New Statesman* of the misery of failing to get the right balance between his work and family life. Much was made of him "killing himself" to leave breakfast meetings at parliament to take his three kids to school, then going back to work in Westminster straight after. As Clegg told one journalist: "I'm very lucky because David Cameron has young children. We agreed the other day we were going to slightly delay the start of the cabinet meeting to allow us both to take our children to school, which is a reflection – if any was needed – of the fact we are both of the same generation in this new politics." The Cleggs too have a nanny, as well as what his wife called "a lot of shadows behind me making my life possible".

And how did we reward these political role models who were showing how even the most important, hectic and high-profile jobs in the country didn't exclude a hands-on attitude to children, even babies? We criticised them for trying to mix work and fatherhood.

Clegg in particular – because he in particular made much stock of trying to balance work and childcare, rather than doing both on top of each other which is the picture Cameron preferred – received nationwide criticism for putting his family above his responsibilities. Particularly after his wife Miriam González Durántez, a high-profile lawyer in her own right, gave an interview to *Grazia* magazine in which she mentioned sharing childcare responsibilities with her husband.

"Nick Clegg should run the country, not the kids to school," decried *The Telegraph*.[4]

Both Nick Clegg and his (Spanish) wife endured a week of media criticism for not putting the country first. Ms Durántez in particular received stick for not stepping up to the plate on behalf of the British nation, and doing what the second-deputy lady (or whatever she's called) should do: take over every aspect of the childcare while her husband helped to run the country.

It's all too easy to quote the antique small-mindedness of the *Daily Mail*, and I could fill this book with examples to illustrate every point in every chapter. I shall just satisfy myself with one comment, verging on xenophobic and definitely misogynist, from columnist Quentin Letts that is worth a laugh at least:

"No wonder he looks so pasty and frayed. It is almost as if he lives in terror of Miriam's fingertips clicking like castanets and summoning him to his housework... Is it really too much to ask that Miriam Clegg temporarily excuse herself from her legal commitments and apply herself to caring for her family and taking some of the stress off Nick? The way things stand, it is hard to avoid the conclusion that our Deputy Prime Minister, at home, is what the Spanish call 'uno calzonazos' — that is, hen-pecked."[5]

The interesting thing about Durántez is that she never promised to play the obedient spouse of a politician. During the campaign she tended not to join Clegg at party conferences, she didn't publicly campaign for him and she didn't do fashion shoots or charity visits.

"I'm the wife of a politician. I don't have a role, I'm just married to him," she told journalists.

Clegg's and his wife's approach to involved fatherhood was simply what they were planning to do anyway – split things a bit more fairly than the norm. In fact, when his first son was born Clegg took extended paternity leave so his wife could go back to work. It was only when it came under public scrutiny that his attempts to play a fairer role became such a big issue. And not in a good way.

Which leaves the debate about parenthood and politics pretty much where it has been since well before 1919, when the first woman was elected to parliament. Instead of asking how parliament and political life should be reformed to accommodate family life, the debate remains about whether those who wish to pursue an active family life should get involved in politics at all. And many women have found the answer is a resounding 'no'. A recent victim was the feisty backbencher Louise Mensch, who retired from a promising career as an MP and Tory media luvvie because, as she wrote to the prime minister, "despite my best efforts, I have been unable to make the balancing act work for our family."

Mensch wanted to spend more time with her children and her husband in New York. Male politicians don't feel the need to retire from politics for the same reason. If they did our reaction would be to call him a pansy want-it-all who couldn't take the pressure (like Nick Clegg is, if the *Telegraph* and *Daily Mail* are to be believed). When a woman resigns to spend more time with her family, it means just that. When a male politician does the same, it's taken as a euphemism for alcoholism, poor mental health or something more untoward. That it could actually be true is unthinkable.

Cameron and Clegg may have made much of their own involved fatherhood, but they have done little to improve the working culture of which they are part. A work-life balance remains a laughable idea for any man, or woman, who wants to work in parliament. They may be in the process of introducing what they call a family-friendly agenda, particularly through flexible parental leave (which I tackle in a later chapter), but neither has yet done anything to change the working or the social culture around the very politics they lead.

Why should male bankers, or academics, or factory workers, or managers, or chief executives try to play a more active role in their children's lives if the new fathers we elected as our leaders get vilified for demonstrating involved fatherhood themselves, and the women politicians who do try to balance their working life and home life so visibly fail to manage it?

So our search for role models continues. Perhaps we should look to the men we pay to be responsible for our children? The truth is there aren't many of them. One in four primary schools don't have any male teachers at all, and only just over one in ten primary school teachers is a man. An adult male in a pre-school or nursery setting is an even less frequent sight, with just 48 men working in state nurseries in the whole of England.

Apart from in the mythical north London media world, where 'mannies' are apparently in as healthy abundance as hummus and biscotti, men just don't tend to work with young children. Ask yourself: would you hire a fully grown adult male to babysit your little ones? Would one even apply for the job? A BBC Radio 2 discussion programme filled a half-hour phone in segment about whether men should even be *allowed* to be nursery assistants at all, given the whole male propensity to abuse children and everything.

What man would want to work with children when the open assumption is that you are at best a bit gay, and at worst, a paedophile? It's worth noting that the most high-profile scandal concerning paedophilia in a nursery in recent times actually had a woman, Vanessa George, as its key protagonist. It was she who was taking photos of children she abused at a nursery in Plymouth, yet no Jeremy Vine phone-in questioned whether women in general should be allowed to look after our kids. The media conclusion was, of course, that it was a male contact on Facebook who cajoled her into taking the pictures, so it *was* the man's fault after all.

We are trapped in a cycle of seeing no man getting on with the job of childcare – or if they do, they're regarded as freaks or heroes, celebrated or vilified by the media, or potential paedophiles. None of this encourages men to get more involved in the lives of our babies, and so the cycle continues. If other men don't do it, or get this kind of reception when they do, what's in it for us?

But even that is perhaps to express a thought most men and a lot of women don't even have. We don't see other men caring for babies, so equal parenting doesn't even occur to us as something that we *could or should do*. With no knowledge or inspiration to work with, the very idea is invisible.

I'm assured by women and men I have spoken to that seeing men successfully and happily caring for children does have an influence on them. My wife tells me that the women in her social networks are impressed and a little jealous of our set-up. Once the surprise and misfired questions – *how could you let him choose what clothes they wear? But he doesn't know how to wash whites and colours separately, does he?* – are out of the way, they declare themselves a little more inclined to try the same in their own homes.

Apart from a few exceptions, women I speak to don't tend to talk in depth to me about equal parenting. Instead, they raise their eyebrows over my version of the story. Man's definition of equality doesn't always chime with a woman's, so I don't blame them for their scepticism. But one way or another, friends, colleagues and others have used our attempt at an equal arrangement to at least analyse their own approaches. If they can do it, people ask themselves, why can't we?

They may not go for the whole equal parenting package. But the man might begin to do things he never before desired to do or thought he was capable of, and which his wife never thought possible. She may roll her eyes as he ostentatiously does something she's been doing without thanks since baby came along, but at least it's a start. Small steps like these are how cultural change is created.

When we see other blokes doing stuff we kinda get the feeling we ought to be doing, we're more willing to try it for ourselves. And when we do eventually do it, we don't quite feel like the freaks we thought we would.

* * *

Overhearing a pair of women speaking outside school recently, I heard one telling the other that she was off to a friend's for two nights. She was leaving a list of things for her husband to do: what time to drop the kids off at pre-school, what to make for dinner, what time school finished, when to get the bath run.

"It's the only way he'll remember what needs to be done," she said. "I won't expect any washing to get done, of course, but at least the kids will get to school on time. At least I hope so."

"Is yours any good at all that?" she asked her friend. It was as if her husband was some kind of possession, a car that can be made to work better if only it's driven well by its female owner.

Or as another pregnant friend wanted to put it when asked "is your husband any good?": yes, of course he's "good". I wouldn't have married him if he wasn't "good".

The daddies on the bus — at least in the unreconstructed version — go *shh shh shh* to the noisy children, who are clearly ruining his journey into town. (I have a wonderful female friend who simply would not allow her mums' group to sing this verse, and that was even before her husband took over the care of their three children full-time.)

It might seem petty to object to idle talk like this. But language is also important. Men talking about women in a dismissive or derogatory way does harm to women, even if they're not actually present, because it creates specific assumptions and atmospheres in which women have to function. In the same way, the chances of men doing a fairer share of childcare are done no favours by this kind of ongoing, drip-drip-drip negative language about their capabilities.

But men themselves are guilty too. Otherwise intelligent, confident men post these kinds of updates on Facebook:

> *"She's letting me do the feeding tonight, so it's going to be messy."*

> *"I'm looking after the kids this weekend, which can only mean one thing: cartoons."*

> *"She's gone out with a friend, which means I'm babysitting."*

They are, of course, having a laugh at their own incompetence, at their own expense. But comments like this betray an embarrassment among men about having a rare go at childcare. Just in case I get it wrong, I might as well start out by announcing I'm bound to screw it up. That way I'll get a laugh out of it, too.

Very rarely are men out-and-proud childcarers. Very rarely do men say (or indeed post) positive things about their own capabilities with their children, even though many are of course excellent hands-on fathers. Rarely do men say, publicly, that fathers are perfectly capable, competent or even good at looking after children. And much less do they challenge negative language and stereotypes used about male childcarers.

However throwaway they are, these comments do matter. Because, in such an atmosphere of negativity and embarrassment, which bloke would want to buck the trend? Take it from me, it's no fun being the exception and still to have to listen to women talk about fathers in that way.

The symbols and signs we see around us every day are no more welcoming or encouraging of men being fathers or carers of babies. At this book's Facebook page, I've started a collection of lazy signs, posters and symbols which link women with childcare, to the exclusion of men. Whether it's the billboard advertising a café that states 'Mums and Toddlers Welcome', the poster for the 'Mothers and Babies' group, or even the sign on the door of the baby-change which pictures a figure in a skirt leaning over a baby, these are subtle reminders that babies are women's business, not men's.

Again, I could be accused of being petty. Everyone knows by 'Mums and Toddlers' the café means parents. Everyone knows that symbol of a woman leaning over a baby means baby-change, not women's baby-change. It's not done on purpose. But even subtle messaging like this can be off-putting, just as a pub that advertised itself with pictures of half-naked women might be off-putting to women.

I'd never go into a café that said 'Mums and Toddlers Welcome', any more than a Christian would go into a community centre that said 'Muslims welcome' – implying, however unintentionally, that other religions aren't. Those prayer rooms at airports aren't advertised with a Christian cross or Jewish menorah in the hope that, by seeing the symbol, we kinda get the idea that the airport authorities mean 'just all religions really'.

The key point is the same as for most issues around political correctness. It doesn't take much to write on a poster or a sign *parents* welcome, instead of *mums*. It doesn't take much to use a symbol of a baby in a nappy, instead of a woman bending over a baby, to indicate nappy change. It may take the tiniest bit of thought and the smallest amount of effort, but the results can be huge and significant. It does no harm to get it right, but a lot of harm to get it wrong. If we want men to play a larger role with their babies, isn't it worth that little bit of extra thought?

And while we're on the subject of language, what's the deal with all this talk about 'the breadwinner' anyway? Couples today don't talk about one being the breadwinner, and the other being the homemaker. What is this, the 1950s? What does that make the lower-earner's income: pin money? With 'breadwinner' come heaps of associations about being the head of the family, being the decision-maker, being solely responsible. These days families tend to have varied earnings, with men and women's income changing, swapping over and complementing each other, at different times in their relationship.

This language around breadwinners and homemakers – only ever used by journalists trying to express a complex world in idiotically simplified language – does none of us any favours. It suggests there always has to be a single person who earns the most, and therefore is champion over all he or she – but mostly he – surveys.

But let's be honest. It's men and women ourselves that perpetuate this language, and the stereotypes behind it. In fact, as I show in the next chapter, we may well thrive on them

7

Women vs men

IT WAS THE biggest bust-up Sarah and I ever had over our children.

It can't have been long after her first maternity leave had finished, and I was looking after Erin for the day while Sarah was working from home. She was on deadline for a TV documentary proposal and must, somehow, have thought she'd get more done stuffed with us into our poky one-and-a-half-bedroom east London flat, than among her coffee-break-taking, water-cooler-gossiping, watching-the-TV-is-working BBC colleagues in White City. It wasn't long before sniping from the sidelines began. I wasn't giving Erin enough attention. I shouldn't do it like that, she prefers it this way. Why don't you read to her? What are you planning to do today? There's a mums' club I usually take her to, why don't you try that?

As the tension grew I felt my every move under scrutiny; in Sarah's eyes I simply wasn't *doing childcare properly.*

Eventually I took the nuclear option. I grabbed my own laptop and my coat and dumped Erin at Sarah's feet.

"Since you're so good at it," I said. "You can do it."

I think I probably slammed the door on my way out. I must have been serious because that night I checked into a dingy hotel in Stratford. This was a pretty brave thing to do: back then, Stratford was far from the gleaming, modern open-plan playground you'll be familiar with from the Olympics coverage. But as Sarah's deadline came and went, I think I made my point. And eventually we made our peace. It wasn't a victory, but we came to an understanding. Sarah has never closely monitored how I do childcare since, and if she does question something I do, she only gives as good as she gets from me in return.

Ask most men what one of their biggest problems with childcare is, and they'll answer: mothers. Women expect us to play our role with the children, but when we try to do it they criticise and instruct, roll their eyes and sometimes shove us out of the way to take over themselves. Just as men unite over a pint to complain about earache from 'er indoors, women find moaning about their partners' incompetence with children a strangely unifying rallying call.

"You have to admit, though," one mother said to me, "women are naturally better at childcare." This attitude is not rare at all. Among friends, from the media and from the baby industry too, we're fed the message that women are natural babyrearers, that they're more suited to the job. And anyway, babies are instinctively happier and more comfortable in the arms of their mothers.

"We love our babies more than men do, they just have to accept that," said another woman to my wife.

But however instinctively right this all feels, like so much guff spouted about childcare it's not actually true. It has been proven for decades that men and women's caring instincts are the same, and there is no innate childcaring ability in women that men lack. In the 18th century, as academic Tina Millar has pointed out, fathers were most often characterised as hands-on, tender, nursing and emotionally involved. In was only into the early Victorian era that such things were regarded as too effeminate for men. According to the Fatherhood Institute, eight in ten women do actually think fathers are as good as mothers at caring for children.[1] Researchers have certainly shown that men's changes in heart rate, blood pressure and skin conductance are just the same as women's when they are around a smiling or crying baby.[2] And that fathers are as sensitive and responsive to their young children as mothers are, if given the opportunity. For example, when fathers feed their young babies they respond appropriately when the baby needs to pause or splutters after taking too much. They also manage to get as much milk into babies as mothers do. Fathers tend to be just as responsive to their baby's bids for attention as mothers.[3]

Fathers and mothers are equivalently anxious about leaving their babies and toddlers in someone else's care. Some researchers have found no differences between levels of maternal and paternal sensitivities during the first year. With four-month-olds, mothers and fathers were equally sensitive, and where there was a difference it was because the mother spent more time with the child, not some innate child-focussed sensitivity.[4]

Similarly, babies are just as likely to become attached to their fathers as their mothers, since they will attach to anyone who responds sensitively to them and provides fun and playful stimulation. And particularly when women aren't around, men frequently pick up and play with their babies, doing exactly the things that are most likely to forge those bonds.[5] In fact, researchers have found that babies do bond as easily with their fathers as with their mothers.[6]

It's not what gender you are, rather what you do that counts.

Let's put all this much more practically and brutally. Men whose wives die in childbirth, or who otherwise find themselves looking after the baby alone from week or even day one, do just fine in their bonding and caring, thanks very much. Like women, these isolated fathers of babies just get on with it and are as good (or as crap) at it as the women around them.

By the way, men get deeply affected too when they do carry out care for their babies, which renders them more nurturing, and raises their levels of hormones associated with tolerance, trust, sensitivity, and even broodiness. The more experienced a man gets in doing this stuff, the more change he experiences.[7] In fact, researchers have found that immediately after the delivery and during the hospital stay, when given the chance, men hold and rock their new babies more than mothers do. Even if that's partly accounted for by the woman being knackered or having wires and drips dangling from her at every angle, it shows pretty clearly that men can be front and centre of babycare from the very beginning, if they're given half a chance.[8]

One friend spoke of how he failed to bond with his baby son when he was born, even going so far as to say he hated his child in those first difficult months. Meanwhile, his wife was busy falling head over heels for their newborn. It's brave of him to confess to this, but it proves nothing about any lack of innate caring or bonding abilities among men. In fact, many women also fail to bond with their babies, and feel exactly the same way about them as my male friend. It's just not talked about very often.

The furore that surrounded the publication of novelist Rachel Cusk's non-fiction book in 2008 about her ambivalence to her own baby, and to motherhood in general, shows just how much of a taboo it is to speak of such things. Yet in review after review of *A Life's Work*, women said Cusk had reflected their own experiences.

Up to 85% of women experience the baby blues in the weeks following labour, but at least one in ten is clinically diagnosed with post-natal depression. A key factor in post-natal depression has been found to be the mother's worries about whether she is bonding with her baby, not feeling she knows what she's doing and society's expectation that motherhood would be rewarding.[9]

In my own experience, the birth and first few months of my daughter's life left me relatively unmoved. She was just a job that needed doing, and didn't offer too much in return, while my wife spoke of a deep love for Erin welling up inside her from the first night. In absolute contrast, particularly because Reid was so reluctant to breastfeed and getting him latched on to the nipple was so bloody painful for my wife, it was Sarah that was left unmoved by our baby son, while my relationship with him seemed to cement right away.

There are all kinds of psychological and cultural explanations that can be offered for our experience, but it certainly belies the idea of a natural instinct for bonding and care among women, that men simply don't have. There are great women parents, but there are also some really appalling ones; just turn to any sensationalist newspaper for intricately detailed examples. Likewise there are some great male child-carers, and there are also some crap ones. Most of us – men and women – sit in the middle somewhere. And when we start, not one of us has the first clue what we're doing.

Women don't know by some biological hocus pocus how to comfort and reassure their babies. They don't automatically divine how much and how often to feed, or whether that cry means boredom or overstimulation, tiredness, teething or time for a nappy change. They learn these things by being thrown in at the deep end. Soon it becomes second nature, and we mistake that for innate ability.

Meanwhile, men rarely get or take an opportunity for this learning-by-doing at the very earliest stage. The subtle separation between men and women's roles begins on day one. As we saw in an earlier chapter, men are sent home from hospital during those all-important first formative hours. By the time Mum comes home with baby, she's already developed a dozen tricks which Dad doesn't know. Out of lack of sleep and a desperate need to comfort the baby, Mum takes over with the magic she's learned, and Dad doesn't get to practise the black arts for himself.

And that's what my tiff with Sarah was really all about. She'd just had six months of maternity leave to learn for herself how to entertain our daughter during the day. What to do with herself, how to ensure Erin was happy and fulfilled, how to ensure she herself didn't die of boredom or kill herself to escape the tortuous repetition of endless games of peek-a-boo.

She'd come to learn over those months what she was and wasn't capable of doing – checking emails: no; cooking: maybe; cleaning: no; phoning friends: well, with a lot of tolerance on the pal's behalf – during the childcare day. By the time I started doing daytime childcare, she pretty much had it wrapped up. But I was just starting out. These were my first early days, *my* post-labour struggle. I knew the muck and mess of babycare, but what to actually *do* during the long working day with a six-month-old, I hadn't had a chance to work out yet.

I wanted to learn how to be a stay-at-home dad for myself. And – worst of all for Sarah – my way wasn't necessarily going to be the same as hers. Women don't know the best way; they only know their way.

We've all seen and laughed along as a childless man is handed a newborn at a barbecue, only for it to begin crying and for the mum to smile weakly and scoop the baby back up again. (When childless women are handed babies pretty much the same happens, unless the woman has lots of mum friends and knows a few tricks of her own. But we look on those women with pity, rather than amusement.) In those situations I find myself thinking: hey, give the guy a break. How about allowing him a few more minutes, even 20 minutes, with your baby? Let him try a few different holds, a few bounces or songs. After all, that's how *you* learned to keep the baby happy. And you didn't have 12 spectators standing round you with fists full of hotdogs and bottles of beer.

My wife was at a female friend's house for coffee, and her husband was milling around too. Perhaps knowing about our set-up, when the baby needed a change, the man stood up without a word and took the baby upstairs. As the two women continued the conversation for a few minutes more, my wife's friend would occasionally snatch a glance up the stairs, clearly wondering why the baby was continuing to cry in the room above. After a few more minutes, she could take it no more and shouted: "Is everything all right up there?"

Dad came down, holding a naked baby in his arms, looking forlorn: "He keeps wriggling," he said. His wife rolled her eyes conspiratorially at my wife in a 'men, huh, what can you do with them?' kind of way. She then snatched up the baby and headed upstairs herself.

In homes the length and breadth of the UK, this little story plays itself out at nappy time, meal time, playtime, work time, bath time and bedtime. Men are giving up too easily, because they know women will do it for them. And women are too willingly taking over, while rolling their eyes at our incompetence.

The result is an atmosphere where men who have learned to do childcare are regarded with suspicion and scepticism, or at the very least surprise. "I'm really impressed that you brought the kids to the barbecue by yourself," said one friend to me. A mother at the pre-school gates took me aside and asked in a sympathetic voice how I was coping, what with Sarah abroad filming for a few days. The (unspoken) response to both being: well, this is pretty much what I get up to every second day of the week. And I'm really only doing what women have been doing for the last, well, forever.

So, why don't women leave men to learn about childcare for ourselves, to make our own mistakes and to work our own way through – like they had to? One answer is that childcaring and homemaking sometimes becomes the only identity mothers have remaining. Their childless friends don't seem to come around so often, their careers are on hold if not in the dustbin, their own interests and hobbies are long forgotten in favour of those of a three-month-old.

As any baby carer knows, just getting through the day intact – or even out of pyjamas – can be a feat in itself. Childrearing is a job for which mothers rarely receive recognition or praise. They don't get the personal assessment or feedback they used to get at work, or even an Employee of the Month award if they've had a particularly good few weeks. I know all this, because it's exactly what I've experienced too.

At the end of a long day, they often have nothing to show for their toil but the same relatively tidy house their partners left that morning. The house may have been to hell and back during the day, and it may have taken all her strength, courage and determination to resurrect it, but her achievements are greeted not with a medal, but with a mere "how was your day, darling?" at best or at worst, "God, I've had a tough one at the office… is dinner ready?"

But there's something else too. There are many great things about spending whole days with your baby. Aside from the difficult times, there are loads of precious times too. The little smiles, the fun, the sheer simplicity and joy of forging a loving, unbreakable and amazing bond with something so small, so dependent and so beautiful. This, perhaps, is the reward mothers get at home, but miss out on elsewhere. It's no surprise then that women become protective of the domain they have discovered themselves in charge of. The job of childcare becomes their expertise, and they chide men's bungling attempts to imitate what they have perfected. It becomes an unwelcome male interference in their new identity.

And I imagine, only because I've felt such things myself, women get really quite jealous when their partners experience joy and smiles from their babies at the end of the day, without having put in much of the hard work for the last ten hours. Perhaps women don't really want men to be able to quieten their babies at barbecues, because what would that say about them as mothers? Women want to be called on to help when their husbands bungle the nappy change, because that shows they're the professional (and he's an idiot).

Isn't there perhaps a slight sense too that, after enduring pregnancy and the pains of labour, some women feel they've *earned* a better, stronger, more instinctive relationship with their child? Men shouldn't have that because we didn't put up with squeezing it out of our nether regions?

It's a game that is doomed to repeat itself. Because it's a game that, despite the slagging off we receive from women behind our backs, men are pretty happy to play along with. It gives us the perfect excuse to keep babycare at arm's length, and to avoid what most of us are actually pretty glad we don't have to do. We may claim to have the tough life going out to work every day and missing our children, but do we secretly know that childcare is the harder deal? It's all too easy to hold up a naked baby and say he's too wriggly when we know our wives will take over and we'll get out of the nappy change. It's all too easy to say the baby settles best with you, so you might as well get up in the night, when it means we get to sleep through and wake fresh in the morning.

We might not say it aloud, but these little tricks are how we function. I like to think of myself as an equal father, but I'll hold my hands up and say I still use a little of this subterfuge to get out of things I don't want to do. My wife, of course, sees the ploy for what it is, because she uses the same tactics on me. Perhaps if I hadn't stormed out that time, I might get away with it more often.

When I look back on that incident, I'm now embarrassed to say I was only doing what men always do. I got an extra day's office work and a nice quiet hotel sleep out of it, and all I suffered in return was sulking from an incredibly angry wife. It was a coward's response. A blown up version of the guy whose baby was too wriggly.

The stronger position would have been for me to say: if you don't like what I'm doing, then go and work somewhere else. Today my business is childcare, and you're interfering in (indicating our crappy little flat) my place of learning and work. It's difficult enough, and your being here is making it worse.

If we're going to make fairer parenting a reality, then we – men and women alike – need to call a truce and we need to toughen up. We need to forget what our parents told us, ignore most of the childcare books, and give each other sufficient space and encouragement to get on with it for ourselves. For women, that means leaving men to get on with childcare, even if it's painful and difficult for you to watch.

We care deeply about our children, and most of us – like you – would never do anything purposefully to put them at risk. Dressing them in non-matching outfits, or forgetting to pack their cuddle bear for a day out, is not going to end in their demise (though the latter might half-kill us). And given half a chance, we'll learn the hard way – just like you did – why not checking the nappy bag before we leave the house can be a mistake. Hey, we might even learn that some things we all think are so important don't matter at all.

If women want men to be active, involved fathers, they have to take a step back when it's our turn. And you do have to let us to take our turn. Women also have to understand that if you want a fairer parenting set-up, you can't behave like you have some ultimate deciding vote over all issues regarding our children. (Meanwhile, chaps, we have to realise that using the 'well, you wanted a baby more' argument really becomes quite low when you've both actually gone ahead and had a child together.)

Sarah once announced the kids were going to stay at their grandparents for the night, because she needed to get up early to go somewhere close by. It wasn't the going to Granny's I objected to: it was that in our apparently equal parenting relationship she hadn't consulted me about where our children were going to spend the night. But this kind of thing goes on all the time: women make decisions about their kids, without consultation or reference to their father, then complain dad doesn't involve himself enough. And our relationship wasn't supposed to be like that.

Women, you also need to be a little tougher on the blokes. You need to be able to go out of an evening and say to the man in your life: you're in charge, so see you later. Then you have to back it up by not calling or texting home to check up on him, or returning early just in case. One woman I know spoke of how in a pub for a girly night out, a friend left early because she was afraid her baby might wake up and her husband wouldn't know what to do. If she'd stayed, he might just have surprised her with his competence. Or at least she might have returned too pissed to notice.

In fact, while you are in the pub with your girlfriends, and they're rolling their eyes about how useless men are, why not put in a good word for your bloke who is actually quite decent at childcare?

And men, we have to be a lot tougher too. We have to man up in our women's work. Instead of looking for the easy way out, we have to persevere with things we don't think we're any good at. We have to be willing to learn on the job, to overcome challenges ourselves, and not to retreat to the all-too-easy option of handing baby back to mother. Not knowing how to do it was what the internet and YouTube were invented for. The more we learn this stuff, and the more we do this stuff, the easier it really does become. And the earlier we get involved – right from birth, if midwives will let us – the sooner we'll get good at it. It becomes second nature to us as well as our wives.

One fed-up mother told me that, on a weekend trip to a museum, her husband went and sat in the café while she chased their boy around the exhibits. The dad, poor chap, said he was tired and bored. He'd wait there until his wife and child were ready to go. God help this guy if he had to look after his child day after day. With childcare, you can't just check out because you're not having fun. Looking after children can be one of the most boring, inane and dissatisfying things we do, but it's part of the deal.

I've been so driven to despair by boredom that I've piled mine into the car and just driven around the countryside until tea time. Anything to get out of the house and do something that wasn't the zoo or the library yet again. Just like with the practical elements of childcare, we have to learn how to cope with the boredom and dissatisfaction for ourselves. When we lived in east London, I took Erin to every single gallery, museum and attraction in the capital, as much for my benefit as for hers. I just couldn't stand a full childcare day at home. I also took my just-learning-to-walk baby to a beer festival with my dad, where with her stumbling, round tummy and wobbling gait, she fitted right in.

But, guys, we also need to be tougher on the women in our lives. We have to demand the time and space to become good at childcare. Even if they say they *want* to stay at home, or choose the clothes, or make the dinners, we need to be able to say: tough, this is an equal deal, and I'm in charge today. And this is where it really gets hard: even when women say they'd rather give up their careers or social life than see us muck things up or do it wrong, we still have to stand our ground and tell them we have a right to be responsible for our children in our own way. And that they're just as likely to *do it wrong* as we are. But then we too have to follow through by actually learning to do this stuff well, and not giving up when it gets hard. And definitely by not expecting a medal at the end.

My wife and I don't argue that much about childcare, but we don't see eye to eye on every aspect either.

She thinks I check my emails too much when I'm with them, play the radio too loud and am too quick to snap at them. I think she doesn't give the children enough space for unstructured play, that she stresses over aspects of their lives that I think really don't matter, and that she doesn't snap at them enough. The difference is that neither of us thinks we are naturally or innately better, and neither of us automatically gets the final say. Freed from a casting vote, we're able to discuss, find a compromise, or agree to disagree. We realise that there isn't a right or wrong way in every aspect of childcare, and that being closer to fair is a greater prize than striving for perfection.

But isn't this a recipe for combative parenting? A battle of wills, where every aspect of childcare is argued over, and then men and women go and do it their own way anyhow? I think the opposite. It allows for a more equal relationship that benefits both parents, while also bringing variety and benefit to the child. There's no doubt that men and women do bring different things to the table in childcare. Mothers tend to do more hugging, soft speaking and repeating with their babies, while fathers provide more verbal and physical stimulation, patting them and using sharp bursts of sound.[10] These differences should be celebrated, not battered out of us. I love messing around in the vegetable patch with the kids, showing them how to dig up worms and how to harvest the beans, talking about how plants grow. Sarah would rather be cooking with them, getting them to try different foods and talking to them about how food makes our bodies get bigger.

We bring different things to the table, enjoy ourselves, and our kids benefit into the bargain. The problem is that men aren't coming to the table often enough, and when they do their contribution is too easily belittled or swept aside.

If nothing else, when men see what it actually takes to look after a child day after day, perhaps we'll be more willing to say thank you when we come in from our work to find the house relatively free of chaos. Just as long as you women do the same for us.

★   ★   ★

Pinned to the inside door of the cupboard where we keep our packets, tins, breakfast cereal, coffee and tea, strategically placed so that Sarah and I see it every single day of our lives, is a list of major housework jobs that need doing.

I think I stuck it up there about two years ago, in a fit of efficiency which stretched only as far as getting out a marker pen, some paper and Blu Tac, and writing down what needed to be done. Clean out the fridge. Brush under the dishwasher. Scrub the skirting boards. Clean the kitchen cupboards. Wash the cooker hood. That kind of thing.

Only one of them has actually been completed since. There's a proud red line scratched through "defrost the freezer". Though that was so we could fit some food in for a Christmas party in late 2011. I'm pretty sure it needs doing again by now.

Since day one, Sarah and I have taken a pretty student-like attitude to housework. If it's not green, it's clean. If parents are coming to visit, scrub, vacuum and dust visible surfaces like mad for an hour before they arrive. Often when guests are coming up the drive, I'll still be in the toilet – the one place in the house where you can do some last-minute cleaning behind a locked door.

When I started mentioning to women friends that I was planning a book on equality in parenting, many of them begged me desperately: "God, you're going to write about housework, aren't you?" Many women, it seems, are more bothered that men don't run a Hoover round or unstack the dishwasher occasionally, than that men don't play a hands-on role with the children.

And they're right. Childcare responsibility is so intimately connected in our social stereotypes of gender roles when it comes to who does the housework and looking after the home, it's impossible to tackle the two separately. Being a good homemaker is what a woman is *supposed* to do, and that invariably includes doing the childcare, while being a good breadwinner, and paying for the home the woman looks after, is what a bloke is *supposed* to do. If a bloke has never stuck on the washing in his life, he's hardly likely to start doing so once a baby comes along.

Nevertheless, if the media like to paint a picture of an attentive father wiping his baby's nose or ring-a-ring-a-rose-ing with his toddlers, they just love the idea of the househusband. Any excuse to use some awful photo library image of a man in a pinny or in washing-up gloves, and that's another Sunday supplement double-page spread taken care of.

"It's official, housework makes men happier," chirps *The Independent*, accompanied by a picture of a man in a girly apron doing the cooking.[11] (Do women actually wear aprons – girly or otherwise – to do the housework?)

"Fathers are happier when doing more housework, says study," joins in *The Guardian*.[12] Their picture? A man holding a baby in one arm, the nozzle of a vacuum cleaner in the other.

Nothing dispels the myth of the new fatherhood more than the simple fact that men aren't doing significantly more housework now than they were decades ago. Men may be doing slightly more childcare, but this rise in hands-on fatherhood has certainly not been matched by men doing more of a share of the household chores – and that includes housework directly related to babies and children. In fact, men without children are more likely to do a fairer share of housework.

ONS research on how we spend our time is devastating to the idea of the new father dutifully doing his fair share of the housework, as well as his share of the childcare. The amount of time spent by men on childcare has increased since 2000, the research shows, but then so has women's. Yet men's time doing housework has actually reduced in the same period.[13] The much-vaunted hands-on father may indeed be just about emerging from mythical status. But the fully paid-up househusband, so beloved of our journalists, belongs firmly with the fairies and unicorns. An easy idea to write about, but extremely challenging to find in actual existence.

Analysis by the IPPR think-tank revealed eight out of ten married women do more household chores than their husbands. Only one in ten married men does an equal amount of cleaning and washing with his wife.[14] According to the Equal Opportunities Commission, mothers spend three times as much time as fathers on household upkeep and food management during the week, and twice as much as men on weekends.[15] Another survey by the Centre for Time Use at Oxford University concludes that men spend half as much time on domestic duties, compared with women. It will be 2050 before equality is achieved when it comes to household chores, the study concludes.[16]

A clear picture emerges. One of men doing a slightly larger amount of spending *time* with their children than they used to, while their wives continue to do the bulk of the childcare-related housework: washing the baby's clothes, making the meals, clearing up the house, changing the sheets, doing the ironing.

Even among involved fathers, it seems, men are doing the nice bits of childcare: the stories, the games, the painting, the rolling around the house creating mess. Meanwhile, women come home from a day at work to do the father's share of the child-related housework. When men go out to work, they don't return the favour. He returns from a hard day at work, then either relaxes or once again takes the nicer bits of childcare – the bath time, the story reading, the tucking in – to give Mum a break. Except she doesn't get to sit on the sofa with a G&T: she's scrubbing congealed rusks out of the creases in the high chair and retrieving stacking toy pieces from every corner of the living room. But at least these men are doing *something*. What more can women ask for?

It's important to make a distinction between childcare-related housework, and other housework. My dad used to come in from work smelling of beer after a day 'doing deals' in the Great Western pub behind Wolverhampton train station. He'd run his finger along the dusty mantelpiece, ostentatiously demonstrating to my mum that the house wasn't as clean as he thought it should be, what with her at home all day with only four children to look after. If I instinctively thought it was a bit mean when I was younger, I'm nothing less than embarrassed now I have my own children.

In the early days of sharing childcare, my wife and I used to apologise to each other when we walked through the door from work. We'd been at home all day, but the house was often a mess, no vacuuming had been done, and the washing was still in the machine. If there was dinner in the oven, that was a good day. Anyone who spends time with children will know the battle it can be to merely maintain the household state of *mess*, and not let mess turn into *chaos*. Out of pure self-interest, it didn't take Sarah and me long to conclude that good childcare wasn't about these other household jobs. The priority every day was to ensure the children were happy, entertained, fed. And relatively clean. Everything else we'd split up when they were in bed, or we'd add to the list on the back of the cupboard door.

But all the evidence suggests that most men – even those doing childcare – do neither childcare-related household chores, nor the non-childcare housework. Far from being househusbands, even today's new fathers are acting like glorified babysitters.

"The revolution in gender roles is unfinished business," says Nick Pearce, director of IPPR. "Women still shoulder the overwhelming burden of household tasks, particularly after they have had children."

The most recent ONS survey of how we spend our time shows clearly that where women are not working or doing childcare they tend to fill it with catching up on a few chores, whereas men spend their spare time doing things for themselves: computer games, hobbies. Men stuff. Amongst unemployed men, the disparity is the largest. Men without jobs do far less housework than even men with full-time jobs, and they fill far more of their spare time with unspecified 'me' activities. For unemployed women, the opposite is true: more housework, more childcare, and less 'me' time.[17]

A friend's husband says he needs at least three hours of 'me' time every day, just to help him express his masculinity. In his case, that means collecting, painting and playing with fantasy figures from *Star Wars*. It takes all sorts.

It is clear that housework is a revealing microcosm of our general approach to men and women's roles in childcare. Women do more of the housework, and prioritise it over their own interests. Men do less housework and it is less of a priority to them than their hobbies. Men say they're rubbish at housework and will only muck it up if asked to do it, whereas women just seem to have the 'knack' for putting the washing machine on at the right temperature. Men expect women to tell them what to do, instead of taking the initiative and doing it themselves without prompting. Like childcare, the woman (willingly or unwillingly) is overseer of what needs to be done, and doles out a small share to the reluctant husband.

If men don't do housework to women's exacting standards, they get it in the neck and so don't bother. And that means the woman takes over and does it anyway. In some cases, men will pay for someone else (another woman) to come in and do the housework that they're unwilling to do themselves. It's the same middle-class male's killer blow when it comes to childcare: I'll pay for more childcare, so you can go back to work (but reduce my own working hours? What a ridiculous suggestion!).

But wouldn't men taking up a much larger bulk of the childcare, particularly during the working day, by *necessity* lead them to doing a fairer share of the household chores? Like inequality over childcare, having to do the bulk of the housework is one of the things that makes women most unhappy about their relationships and work-life balance.[18] And it is, of course, a key thing – next to money – that couples argue about. A more equal partnership in childcare could not only lead to a fairer housework deal, but reduce tension at home too.

To be honest, I can't get too worked up about the housework. (And what woman hasn't heard that from her partner?) In my defence, my wife shares the same healthy scepticism. As with childcare, most men could do a lot more of the chores – and those men who already claim to be equal in childcare should take a critical look at the share of housework (child-related or otherwise) they actually do. But likewise, women could turn the importance and standards dials down a notch or two. Then we'd all probably be a little happier. And please, journalists, no more pictures of househusbands in pinnies.

Anyway, according to one European study, doing housework makes men happier (either because it makes us feel good or because we get a quieter life as a result). The same survey showed where men took on a bigger share of the household burden, women's happiness levels were also higher.[19] And according to a study by Lancaster University for the charity Working Families, men who do the majority of the housework say they have the best work-life balance overall, in contrast to those men who pay someone else to help with the domestic chores, who were more likely to be troubled by their work-life balance.[20]

When I'm on a childcare day, I put a wash on, prepare the meals, clean up after ourselves, put some clothes away. And yes, I do decide (by myself!) what my own children wear, help them to get dressed and stick whatever they wear in the wash when it gets dirty. On Sarah's days, she'll do the same. At the end of each day, once the kids are in bed, we'll both spend 20 minutes or so together putting the house back upright, or we'll take it in turns. Often, if someone has been at work all day, they'll do bath and bedtime then the after-hours clean-up, while the main childcarer of the day goes for a run, catches up on emails or goes for a drink with friends. In our house, childcare is the tough job. It trumps a day at the office anytime.

I hope we've ended up with a relationship based on wanting to do our fair share, and on wanting to help each other, rather than one based on continually trying to wriggle out of jobs that need doing. We don't always get it right, but we decided within weeks of moving in together that life was way too short to argue about the washing up.

And, of course, we take turns. We take it in turns to scribble things on that list on the back of the cupboard. And then we strictly and religiously take turns to put off or completely ignore the things we've written up there.

8

It's all work work work

WHEN THE PHONE rang, I already knew what it was about.

It was 2004 and that late-20s period in our lives – pre children – when Sarah and I were both working long hours, drinking with colleagues and friends most nights, and loving every minute of it. It was perhaps two or three days after the South Asian tsunami; the full devastation of the disaster was beginning to emerge as aid agencies and journalists arrived on the scene. The night before the call, Sarah had come home late from work, full of ideas for a news documentary about the disaster, concentrating on local angles and how charities were responding. So when she phoned the next day, there really was only one thing she was likely to say.

"I'm booked on a plane to Sri Lanka," she said from a taxi on its way to Heathrow. "I don't know when I'll be back. But I'll try to text you when I arrive, but you know...

what with the electricity being off, I probably won't get a signal. OK? Gotta go, bye...".

Sarah was a researcher, then assistant producer, then producer on BBC *Panorama* as well as other investigative documentary strands. BBC through and through – she'd worked her way up from the corporation's training scheme – hers was the kind of job that meant she always kept her passport on her, and a toothbrush at work. She loved the rush of frontline journalism, particularly making important films on social issues. Her idea of a good time was to work 48 hours straight, mainlining coffee and takeaways on one of the legendary *Panorama* 'fast turnarounds', following a disaster or important breaking news story. And she was really good at it.

In her journalism career, Sarah has flown to New Orleans following hurricane Katrina, chased – and been chased by – Scientologists across the east coast of the United States, exposed from the inside the money-making cult of Kabbalah (which counted Madonna among its followers), revealed the devastating side-effects of anti-depressant drugs, and highlighted – time and again – the cases of families robbed of their babies after being wrongly accused of shaking or twisting them. She's also done less exciting documentaries about the economy and micro pigs.

With undercover work and the door-stepping of crooks particular specialities, Sarah's career was high octane, exciting, very time-consuming and highly rewarding, including some actual TV gongs. So when she called me about Sri Lanka, the excitement in her voice was no surprise. This passion was exactly one of the reasons I'd fallen for her in the first place.

We already knew each other from a campaign organisa- tion I worked for, and we'd got it together drinking Italian beer around a campfire at the G8 protests in Genoa, Italy in 2001. She was there drumming up a story on the activist movement and I was, well, I was part of that movement. It may sound like a tall tale, but during one particularly fraught march to the G8 summit, we rescued each other from a tear gas attack by the thuggish Italian riot police, helping each other over a fence and running hand in hand for our lives through the acrid smog. We seem to have been holding hands ever since.

And I was proud of my wife, even if it did mean being stood up more than I would have liked, or her disappearing into editing studios week after week. She was changing the world, one TV programme at a time, and loving every moment of her career into the bargain. Though I would joke about her having a BBC chip installed, good TV journalism really was what she was all about. Then, just to fuck it all up, came babies.

It turns out you can't be a high-octane, sleep-at-work, drop-everything-at-the-last-minute-and-fly-to-Syria documentary producer if you have a wailing, feeding infant that needs your attention almost every minute of the day. Or at least not if you're a woman.

There's a point in TV – around childbearing age – where most of the women documentary producers, reporters and researchers suddenly disappear. The men stick around because they often have women partners who are willing to be primary carers and to suffer the stand-ups and weeks away their husband's work inflicts. But when we had Erin, Sarah knew she couldn't go back to producing. It's not a career you can do part-time. It's not a career you can do *full-time*. After maternity Sarah started back at the BBC for one, followed by two, days a week. But this time she worked in programme development, a kind of journalistic wasteland where women with young children end up, and where they spend their days thinking up ideas for programmes, but not actually doing any of the good, exciting and rewarding stuff like actually making TV. And here's the thing: she was grateful.

She could stay in the BBC and journalism, sort of; she was still making programmes, kind of; and she got to have children too. If she could just stick it out in programme development for the next 18 years, she might be able to go back into TV producing – just in time to start thinking about retirement. But whatever: at least she got to spend her previously exciting days with two little people who couldn't walk or talk, and certainly didn't know anything about current affairs, so that's OK then. Like for many millions of working women the world over, it slowly dawned on us that – like it or not – Sarah's career would never be the same again. And all we'd done was have a baby.

It was in the context of Sarah's loss of career that my own working life was forced into very clear relief. It challenged me to ask, even though I was an equal parent out of work hours, whether I was doing enough during working hours.

Before we had Erin I was running my own copywriting and publishing business, producing fundraising materials, reports, websites and events for charities. At its height, my company employed six people full-time, a part-time marketing assistant, an administrator and a handful of freelances and contractors. We had the swanky office in charity-centred east London, all exposed brickwork, beanbags, posh coffee and fancy biscuits.

I was working hard, way more than full-time, trying to build something really special and (because we only worked with charities) worthy in its own way. I was earning a reasonable salary doing what I loved: working with words. When Erin came along, was I willing to put my business at risk and work fewer days for the sake of having a baby?

We were committed to parenting equality from the very start outside of work, but it strangely didn't occur to us at first that our working lives had be equal too. We wanted to be fairer, but equal? That, we told ourselves, would never work. We did what other couples do: we fumbled along in new-baby tiredness, with Sarah's maternity leave turning into her being pretty much a full-time mum. When her six months of paid maternity ended, I went down to working four days a week – the most, I argued, my business could spare me. I spent one day a week with our baby, freeing up my wife – for just one day a week – to work in the TV wasteland. My one day a week was far more than any other dad I knew, so at least I was doing something, eh?

It wasn't fair and it wasn't right. It became clear that it wasn't fair as I watched any hope Sarah had of resuming her career turn to dust. Her very working identity had become subsumed by childcare, leaving her a little lost, a lot dissatisfied and definitely miserable. Her passport remained resolutely closed, buried under a huge pile of babygrows and washable nappies.

But what sacrifice had I made for the family unit we'd decided to build together? As I watched her career and sense of independence ebb away, we decided I would increase my childcare time, eventually working exactly the same as my wife, with a nursery filling in the gaps. We ditched nursery as well in the end, and then it really was two-and-a-half days working, and two-and-a-half days childcare a week each.

But I'm getting ahead of myself. Equality in our working lives didn't happen right away; it wasn't a simple process. The new fatherhood myth would have us believe that, if they could, men would jump at the chance to be part-time, equal or even full-time fathers. A quarter of working fathers feel their work negatively impacts on their relationship with their children — hardly surprising when, as I mentioned, nearly one in five has missed four or more significant events in their child's life due to work in the past year. Half of working men have missed at least one such event.[1] Men want things to change, yet they're not changing. Why not?

An acid test is paternity leave. Those very early days of our babies' lives are the ones that are most important both for father-child bonding, and for men to learn the ropes, along with their wives, about what it takes to look after a baby. An involved father in the first few weeks stays involved as the child grows older. If men miss out on this opportunity, then the gulf between father and child, and men's roles and women's roles, begins from day one and gets only wider as roles become more entrenched.

Before April 2011, things were pretty simple in the paternity-leave stakes. Men were entitled to their standard two weeks' paid paternity leave from work. Baby comes, dad rushes home from work and then isn't seen by colleagues for a fortnight. When he returns it's all pats on the back, jokes about his tiredness and baby sick, and before you know it, back to normal. The Labour government proposed paternity leave changes which eventually came into force in April 2011, ushered in by the two new fathers heading up the new Conservative-Liberal Democrat coalition. Supported by all parties, the measure aimed to release women to go back to work earlier, while allowing men to play a stronger role with their new children.

As well as the standard two consecutive weeks' paid paternity leave, fathers in the UK (excluding Northern Ireland, where powers are devolved) can now take up to an extra 26 weeks' paid leave, as long as the mother of the child is not claiming the leave for herself. In other words, there's a block of 26 weeks of paid parental leave that either the man or woman can take. What a release for new fathers, desperate to spend time with their new babies!

Not quite. Even before these new rules were introduced, 40% of fathers said they would not take up the opportunity of the extra paid parental leave. Indeed, only two out of three fathers even take the two weeks' paid paternity leave they've had for years. Almost nine in ten men said they would not take more paternity leave if it was offered to them.[2] Why not?

Affordability is most often cited. Men say they can't afford to take their standard two weeks because of the drop in wages it entails. So they're hardly likely to take half a year with a similar wage drop. Paid paternity or parental leave doesn't mean weeks on full pay. Companies can choose to continue the man's wages at his normal level, but they certainly don't have to. In 2012, the government only repaid the company £135.45 per week for this kind of leave, meaning if a company wants to be generous it has to make up the difference between that and what the man usually receives.

Some companies are happy to shell out for the initial two weeks as a kind of new-baby bonus, though by no means all of them. But very few companies would or could pay the difference between the statutory level and the man's usual pay for 28 weeks in total. In smaller companies it's probably not that they're unwilling to top up even the first two weeks. It's that they really can't afford to do so. With only two or three staff, one body missing can have a massive effect, and paying for agency cover makes budgets even tighter still. It's worth noting too, for those who accuse the self-employed and business owners of having it easy, that if you're self-employed HMRC doesn't reimburse you a penny for your own paternity leave. Taking two weeks to welcome a new baby, let alone another 26 weeks, really does mean receiving no money at all. That was the case with me. Self-employed women, by the way, do get an alternative maternity allowance in place of the statutory maternity pay they would have got from their employers.

No wonder, then, that so many men aren't taking their measly statutory two weeks, let alone any share of the extended leave to which they're entitled. Babies are an expensive thing to have around, so their arrival is not the time to cut back even the most meagre income that can be earned. Yet there is something very wrong when men feel they can't take just a couple of weeks off work to be with, help out and learn how to care for their newborn baby. What kind of society do we live in where employers and governments have constructed a system that financially penalises men who want to play a more active role in their child's first few days of life?

I'm not so naïve as to think this is something that can be solved with the signing of a cheque. As an employer, and an involved father myself, I felt compelled and thankfully able to offer a full two weeks' paternity leave, at normal salary rate, and a further two weeks at half salary to new fathers, even though I could only claim two weeks back at the statutory rate from HMRC. But I won't pretend that I wasn't glad I only had to pay out a couple of times.

As a tiny company run on tight margins, it hurt us. I tried to do the right thing with maternity and sick pay too, but I can admit now that if the three women I employed had all had babies in the same year, my company would probably have struggled to meet even the slightly more generous than statutory maternity pay I'd promised. It's a fact which always makes me smile and shake my head when – even though I like to think of myself as a good few notches to the left of

The Guardian – I hear calls for selfish fat-cat employers to dig deeper into their own pockets to fund more generous paternity and maternity. As if small companies like mine had endless stashes of gold and jewels hoarded away in some kind of charity version of Aladdin's cave. Eight out of ten employers in the UK are like my company was, employing fewer than ten people. Surely, it can't be down to employers alone to persuade men financially to actually take the paternity leave they are, by rights, legally allowed?

But what of government? In her book *Shattered: Modern motherhood and the illusion of equality*, Rebecca Asher makes a very detailed and absolutely convincing case that fairness in childrearing is very far behind what we assume it to be. She calls for government to reimburse companies the full salaries of men on paternity leave, up to a cap for high earners, so loss of earnings is no longer a barrier to taking the legal entitlement. Men should be given seven weeks' paternity leave in the first year on full salary, on a use-it-or-lose-it basis, she argues.

When I first read Asher's book, I experienced a deep twisting in the pit of my stomach. I was planning a book on parental equality, and in the research stage already I'd found someone had, articulately and effectively, well and truly beaten me to it. Once I recovered, I could only heartily concur with Asher's suggestions. But there does seem to be one vital flaw in her argument. Government just isn't going to fund it.

Now I won't pretend to be an economist, but is it any surprise the coalition government won't pay men or women their normal wages during their parental leave, however much they'd like to? The UK has just undergone the deepest recession since the 1920s. Disabled people are having vital life-enabling equipment taken from them, school class sizes are being increased (and new classrooms made smaller), benefits for those out of work are being cut, public service wages are being frozen or cut, people with serious diseases like cancer and multiple sclerosis are being denied the drugs and treatments that they need, and on, and on. The money just isn't there. Even Labour, positioning itself as a spending rather than austerity government, would baulk at such a massive expense for the mere sake of gender equality. Even in boom years, rather than recession, it's doubtful any prospective government would see fully-funded paternity leave as a vote winner.

In May 2011, the coalition government did start to float new ideas for maternity and paternity leave, including that ordinary paternity leave would be increased from two weeks to six weeks, but paid again at the statutory rate. Those six weeks could be taken when most convenient for employer and employee, so not necessarily as soon as the baby is born. Spreading out paternity leave like this allows the man to get to know his baby from the start, but also to keep his hand in at work and take time off when he's really needed, once the baby has properly woken up.

From 2015, men would also get a share of an additional 25 weeks of paid parental leave at the statutory rate, of which 10 weeks could only be taken by the father. If the man didn't take it, it would be gone, effectively forcing men to play a bigger role in childcare, and helping women to get back into the workplace quicker. This is known as the use-it-or-lose-it model. Men would also get paid leave for two antenatal appointments.

However, in November 2012 the government backtracked on what would have been incredibly progressive parental leave policies. Under pressure from business leaders fearing for their bottom lines, proposals on extended parental leave and ring-fenced leave for fathers were significantly, devastatingly, watered down. Disappearing to the same place where children's gloves go, perhaps never to be seen again, went the promised six weeks of paternity leave and the restricted leave that only fathers could take.

Men would not get any more than the same old two weeks' paid paternity leave after all. Fathers would get to share a total of nine months' paid parental leave with the mother of their child, to be divvied up however the parents like, but significantly the fathers' share would not be on a use-it-or-lose-it basis. There will still be no full reimbursement of parental leave pay for companies, which means most men will get only statutory pay for any time they do take off, even those first two weeks, let alone nine months.

Despite being heralded by deputy prime minister Nick Clegg as "a shift to an entirely new system of flexible parental leave", the result will be pretty much business as usual. Men won't take much, or even any, leave because they'll say they can't afford to, and women will take the vast majority of parental leave entitlement just like they always did.

And that means employers will continue to be reticent about employing or promoting women who might just disappear for long periods of time to look after babies, and will be able to pile the pressure on men to not consider playing a fairer part in bringing up their children. As one Conservative MP put it to the BBC: "I used to work in recruitment and there is a kind of assumption that women are a bit of a liability sometimes, to recruit, because they might just go off." In short, same old story.

Nick Clegg has promised to look again at extending paternity leave – for introduction no earlier than 2018 – when the economic conditions might just be more favourable to business. In the meantime, is parental equality to just wait patiently on the side lines?

It seems clear, even with their new right to share parental leave with their wives, men still won't be taking it up in large numbers. Even though women on average earn around the same as men before kids come along, it will remain women who will be left at home with the baby. Parental leave, men say, is unaffordable for them to take. Why, then, is it affordable for the mothers who earn the same as they do?

Can the much-trumpeted progressive societies of Scandinavia, where a more equal arrangement is seen as a key to child and family welfare, as well as economic growth, give us a clue to what is going on? The Fatherhood Institute rates the UK as number 18, out of 21 countries (treating the UK as one legislative body), on its international Fairness in Families Index. Can we learn from our betters?

At the top of the index, in Sweden parents get a share of well over a year of parental leave between them. Crucially, two months of that leave can only be taken by the father – use it or lose it. In Norway, number three on the index, where again just over a year's parental leave is available to share between parents, nine weeks must be taken by the mother, and six weeks can only be taken by fathers. And it works. Men in Sweden and Norway take up their entitlement in droves, with nine out of ten Norwegian fathers taking their extended entitlement, and eight out of ten Swedish fathers.

But scratch the surface just a little deeper, and the model may not be all it's cracked up to be. First, the governments of Sweden and Norway both pay a more generous percentage than the UK of the man's wages while he is on leave. But second, the moment parental leave does become shareable in these countries – rather than earmarked only for the man or the woman – it is the woman who overwhelmingly takes the extra leave. The system is constructed so that men and women have paid, equal access to their children in the first months, but the moment it's optional who the main carer is, mum – or rather *mamma* in Swedish and Norwegian – is the word.

In Iceland, which offers the longest paternity leave in the world, three months is reserved for fathers only. Again it's combined with higher wage replacement, and there's a huge take-up. But once more, when leave becomes shareable with mothers, only one in five fathers takes it. These countries are definitely fairer, but they are hardly utopias of parental equality.

Based on their experience, it's not difficult to guess what the UK coalition government's revised plans to allow slightly more parental leave, but not to earmark any of that leave only for men, is likely to lead to. Here, as in Scandinavia, men will take up their paternity leave when they have to, but are less likely to when they can get away with not doing it. Men say they can't afford it.

Our own paternity leave take-up patterns are indicative. Take the first two weeks a man gets, and now will continue to get after 2015: ordinary paternity leave. It's true that some employers don't top up the statutory pay, leaving men on just £135.45 a week for those two weeks. That's not much, but it is something.

The minimum wage works out at £232.12 for a 37.5-hour full-time working week. Those men on the very lowest full-time incomes, whose employer doesn't top up a penny of their paternity pay, would lose £96 a week for two weeks by taking their paternity leave. Is that really too big a loss for a family to decide it's not worth his taking the time off at all? And that's just the very poorest men. Those on higher incomes would obviously lose more of their usual income during those two weeks, but they are paid more in the first place. And note, if their partner is on maternity leave, she will be receiving her own income too.

Are our families really not willing to drop our earnings –
whether we earn a lot or a little – for two weeks so we can
be with our babies and partners in those first days? Given
the clearly proven longer-term benefits to our children
and our families of men taking their paternity leave, is this
really not something worth shelling out for? It probably is
reasonable to suggest that men on the very lowest incomes
are finding our meagre paternity rates a real barrier to
taking time off work to be with their child. But men who
use this excuse when they earn a lot more are probably
stretching the truth just a little. However reluctant, those
guys seem to find the cash for a £700 or more top-end
baby travel system easily enough.

And for neither working poor couples, nor for working
middle-class couples, do financial barriers answer the bigger
question. Parental leave can be shared between men or
women, and men and women on average earn around the
same before children come along. So why is it still women
who are taking the bulk of the parental leave, while men
are going straight back to work after taking – or not taking
– their initial two weeks off?

I'm not denying that financial barriers are a problem,
but rather highlighting that the solution always seems to be
the man, rather than the woman, going to work; and the
woman, rather than the man, sacrificing her working life for
the children. Perhaps the problem is really something more
deeply rooted in our very working culture.

Are men who want to play a more hands-on role with
children finding both explicit and subtle barriers at work
prevent us from doing what we really want to do? After all,
as the Fatherhood Institute claims, 8% of fathers surveyed
had been told by their employers they were not even *allowed*
to take their paternity leave. That is, of course, illegal.[3]

Management Today is the biggest-circulation management title in the UK, read monthly by nearly 90,000 business managers, executives and owners. In October 2012, a feature by part-time features editor, and new mum, Emma De Vita shone a light on the working world's attitude to part-time working. Even part-time bosses, the article showed, were wary of admitting to working part-time, such is our *only full-time equals full commitment* working culture. A survey quoted in the feature said just over 40% of part-time managers don't admit to it because of the negative stereotype, a quarter because they thought they would be labelled as un-committed, and one in ten because they thought it might curtail their promotion chances.

De Vita interviewed five part-time managers in her piece and only one of them was a man. He, significantly, was the only one whose part-time work had nothing to do with childcare. To be honest, the feature set the bar pretty low for part-time work anyway, with all interviewees working just four days rather than five, and most making up that time in evenings and on weekends.

In a working culture where even senior managers feel they have to hide that they work reduced hours, what chance for men in general to ask for part-time or flexible working so they can do childcare, let alone paid or unpaid time off to attend antenatal appointments and babycare classes? Some men cite a culture in their workplaces of not taking sissy paternity leave, even though they're legally entitled to do so. What next, time off to vacuum the living room?

One stay-at-home father told me: "When people ask you what you do I would never say I'm a stay-at-home dad. It changes the way people talk to you. When people ask, I generally say I'm on a career break. And then I describe what I used to do, even though I've got no intention of going back to that job."

Things work colleagues too often say to men who look after children:

> *"So, she's got you all chained up at home, has she?"*

> *"Off you go, part-timer. We'll just get on with the real work."*

> *"I'd love to do what you do, but – well – I just can't."*

> *"Have you had a crack at any of the playgroup mums yet? I bet you get to see loads of tits."*

> *"I know you're on a day off tomorrow, but I'll just give you a call about the Stevens account around 11, OK?"*

> *"The guys from upstairs want us in a meeting next Tuesday, so if you could just get a babysitter, that would be great."*

> *"I heard dads who do childcare are less sexy to their wives. Can I have your wife's number?"*

Some men cite worries that they'd be passed over for promotion or pay rises if they took paternity leave, and others – those who work for very small companies – say they don't feel able to take paternity leave because it wouldn't be fair on their boss.[4]

It does seem to be true that managers are reluctant to grant flexible working to men, or if they do, they ask men to keep it quiet in case everyone else wants it too. And who can blame the employer who, though they might desire part-time work for themselves, would like the easy life of an office of reliable full-time men, who aren't going to go off for long periods to have babies, costing the company money?

Women do have a legal right to paid time off for antenatal appointments and classes, which men currently don't automatically get, and they should. Under coalition plans, men will get the right to attend two antenatal appointments from 2015. But fathers have exactly the same right to build a case for and then ask for flexible and part-time working as women do. In neither case do employers have to grant it, but in both they are legally obliged to carefully consider it and, if they decline, give reasons.

The fact is that women are asking for part-time and flexible working, and getting it. Men, as a rule, are not even asking. And where men are being refused part-time work, they're certainly not challenging that decision, taking it to a higher level, lobbying through their trade unions or taking their employers to court.

Men seem to be good at asking for pay rises, promotions and extra benefits – in fact, they're much better than women at these things. But when it comes to the right to do child-care, it is us rather than women who are too scared to ask. We're not even making a stink about what's preventing us from asking. Few employers are going to gift part-time or flexible working unless we request it, so if we really want it we are going to have to push just a little. Yet we don't.

There are two things at play here. First is the question of whether men should do more of a share of the childrearing, and reduce or change their working hours accordingly – equality in parenting for the sake of the man. But second is whether our not doing so is perpetuating the pay gap and glass ceiling that women face at work – equality for women's sake.

Women at childbearing age, particularly when they return from maternity part-time, find promotional opportunities greatly reduced. Their male counterparts' salaries begin to proportionally increase more rapidly than theirs. Whether this is due to discrimination by an employer who assumes she won't give her all because of the children, or more subtly because a woman believes she can't offer what's needed for promotion and pay rises because of childcare, the result is the same: a female career slowdown that men don't face.

If you really and honestly believe men make better managers and company CEOs, and should simply because of their gender be paid more than women, then this state of affairs should cause no concern. In fact, I'm not quite sure why you'd be reading this book. If gender equality isn't important, I'm hardly going to convince you parental equality is worth considering.

But if we don't believe gender discrimination at work is OK, then our failure to ask for part-time working, or to sacrifice some of our own working life in favour of our partner's career chances, could be perpetuating exactly the kind of unequal working culture that, to boot, we claim is preventing us from being more engaged fathers.

We end up doing ourselves, our families, our wives, and women in general, no favours at all by accepting that, at work, that's *just the way things* are. And it does nothing to break the vicious cycle that keeps men like us at work and away from our families. Because if we don't get a sniff of flexible hours or part-time work, are we really likely to grant the same as we become managers and CEOs into the future?

There's no other way to cut this: men aren't taking the

opportunity to work less and be with their children more, even though they say they want to. They aren't even asking.

So why aren't men backing up their stated desire to be with children and actually working flexibly or part-time, or even becoming stay-at-home dads? Poor paternity pay, out-dated working cultures and even the legislation are certainly off-putting. But they are far from the whole story. In fact, they offer a convenient excuse and smokescreen that hides a more fundamental problem.

Men aren't reducing their working hours and working part-time or equal hours with their wives because – despite protestations to the contrary – they don't really want to do it.

Put simply: if they did want to do more childcare, they would. Men would be demanding shorter or more flexible hours as part of pay negotiations, or before they agree to take on new jobs. They're not. If employers knew they had to offer childcare-friendly working arrangements to get the best candidates, that would be written into every contract.

Men would be working through trade unions to push for more child-friendly entitlements for themselves and their male colleagues. They're not. There is no trade union cam-paign anywhere in the UK about male parents and working rights. Men would be challenging employers in the sex dis-crimination courts who allow part-time working for female staff, but not for men. They're not. Men, who more or less run the government, the opposition, industry, business, trade unions, charities and the media would be making change happen, and quickly, if they really wanted it. They're not.

For the most part, men get what they want. Men make up 85% of the coalition cabinet, with only two women senior members. Three of the four women in the Lib-Con cabinet at time of writing don't have children.[5] Men make up four out of five members in both the House of Commons and the House of Lords. Three out of every four UK company senior positions are taken by men, with 95% of FTSE 100 companies led by male chief executives or chief financial officers. Half of FTSE 250 companies have no women on their board at all. Some 70% of national newspaper journalists are men, working on papers edited and run by men. Eight out of the top ten newspapers have almost twice as many male editors as female editors.

In our homes, politics, media, industry, it is men making male decisions that get things changed. Despite the work of generations of feminists, it is how much of our society continues to operate.

In her book *The End of Men: And the rise of women*, Hanna Rosin shows that even while outperforming men in a variety of educational and work settings, when it comes to children even senior women managers are left with the struggle to make childcare and their careers work together. "Forget the balance, this is the merge," the author quotes Facebook executive Emily White as saying.

But the problem is still framed as one that women and their employers have to figure out for themselves, "the single most vexing problem for ambitious working women, one everyone thought was unsolvable: how to let them spend time with their children without ruining their careers". The solution, it turns out, is more understanding employers and training women to juggle childcare and work better (so there's less distinction between them – the *merge*), rather than any call on professional or executive men to do a fairer share.

Time and again in professional articles in business magazines and in work sections of our newspapers, the same approach prevails: how to equip women to balance their childcare obligations and careers, as if men don't have any childcare *obligations* to consider at all.

A fairer share of parenting will only come about when men – as well as women – demand it and then do it. And men simply are not demanding it, and they're certainly not doing it. Yet it's something we claim to want more than anything else.

So, the question should really be not why don't we do it, but why don't we *want* to do it?

★   ★   ★

When friends and colleagues get to know about our equal parenting arrangement, it's often that they will say to me: well, it's alright for you, isn't it? You're self-employed. It's easy for you to look after the children when you run your own business, when you're the boss and can choose your hours. Some of us, they think but don't say, actually have to *work* for a living. But I have, of course, also heard the same from freelances, those who are self-employed and others who run their own businesses. This time *their* work situation is the reason why they can't be equal parents. One didn't even take his two-week paternity leave, he said, because he is self-employed.

Everyone thinks they are a special case. The *it's all right for you* argument gets everything the wrong way around. I'm not able to do childcare *because* I work part-time and am self-employed. I chose to work flexibly, work part-time, made sacrifices and shaped my working life like this. And I did it because I wanted – I needed – to play an equal part in childcare.

I used to do a lot of travelling around the UK, to carry out well-paid consultancy and training. It was the travel I had cut down because of the childcare, not the other way around. I, immodestly perhaps, think I might make a pretty good director of communications at a national charity, bringing with it a decent pay packet to boot. But I don't apply, because those jobs aren't usually part-time. What friends see is the result of choices I've made, not a fortuitous accident that I've exploited.

And I admit, it wasn't a painless experience. Sarah did six months' paid maternity leave when Erin came along, after which I began chipping in with my token one day a week as she eased her way back into work. And I did find it tough to reduce my working hours from five to four days a week. On top of the equal non-working-hours stuff I was doing for our new baby, I was trying to complete my business-related work in the evenings too. But slowly I got used to it, my team got used to not being able to call me on a Wednesday, and we struggled through.

One day a week of childcare, I reminded myself (trying to justify my as yet unequal share of the baby work), was more than any other dad I knew. But in truth I was off building my business while Sarah had just one day a week to make her mark at work. She could barely clear a week's worth of emails before lunch, so working one day every seven wasn't much better than not working at all.

We put Erin in a local nursery for two days a week, freeing up Sarah for an extra day at the BBC and allowing me to blissfully continue my four days. The only problem was that Erin hated it, and the reason she hated it was that the nursery was shit.

And anyway, nursery still meant someone had to take Erin and pick her up afterwards, which we shared equally and which meant neither of us would get a decent full day's work done on those days. I ended up getting less work done when I was working. And I was leaving my office early for the nursery pick-up, leaving my team, to whom I was supposed to be showing leadership, continuing to work for another couple of hours at least. (They of course didn't see the extra hours I was doing to make up for it most evenings.)

Now, no one was happy. And we still weren't equal. Equality in our working lives, on top of our non-working childcare equality, only really happened once we'd moved house. Erin started at a new nursery, a good one at which she was happy, for three days a week. For a couple of months Sarah and I both worked four days a week each, and shared the nursery run as we had before.

But by the time baby Reid came along, we'd already decided we didn't want them to be in nursery at all. Others will have differing opinions and priorities, but we'd decided nursery wasn't what we wanted for our children at such an early age, and we decided to change our arrangement yet again. This time, we decided, we would be equal from the start.

I worked four days a week during Sarah's second maternity leave, now used to a shorter working week and welcoming the opportunity for long weekends with our children while they were babies. But when Sarah's maternity was over, I went up first to two days of childcare, then up to two-and-a-half, the same as she was doing. That transition was the most difficult of all. I remember the painful conversations with senior members of my team, who rightly surmised this would mean more work and responsibility for them, but probably without any pay rise to recognise it. It was just as the recession was kicking in, my team were worried about their jobs already and now I was piling more work onto them, while taking more of a back seat myself.

I don't blame them for thinking I was putting my family before the business. I was. I don't blame them for the forlorn cry that emanated when I announced I was reducing my hours yet again: "But what about us?" The truth was I was every bit as unhappy about reducing my days, particularly in those tough economic times. But I decided I had to do it. My wife's career was in the toilet. I needed to at least give her a chance to rebuild it. As painful as it was, I had to sacrifice at least a bit of my work so she could recover a little of hers.

And I had to do my fair share of childcare, first because I really did want to be with my children more and second because it was the right thing to do. We were equal outside working hours, so why not during? In view of what she'd been through, I had no good defence. Is it possible to both regret something bitterly, but know you did the right thing?

Whether it was through the effects of recession, my poor management, or my inability to give my business everything it needed, I don't know. But over a year I gradually found the size of my business had reduced from a six-person company, with all the stresses and conflicts that entailed, to just me and a few freelances. I'm happy to say my old team seem to be doing fine going their own way, so I don't feel too guilty. But I do acknowledge it could have gone the other way for them. It was an incredibly painful experience, but one we all had to go through at least partly because of the choices I'd made and the commitment to equality I had with my family.

My wife gave up most of the choice about the direction of her career when she became pregnant. The whole episode gave me an insight into the painful choices that every working woman is forced to make about her career and children, and which men – often with the consent of women – very often just let them get on with. If anything, it made me even more determined to be an equal father, and to try to generate a culture that encourages and even forces men to play a fairer role.

It's sad that our legislative framework, as well as the *can't do* attitudes of most men and employers, creates situations like these. But until the framework offers a more level playing field for men and women, men need to take a fairer share of the sacrifice. If we don't, then our wives will continue to take the lion's share on themselves.

Is that really what we want? Every time we men consider the effect reducing our working hours would have on us, our happiness and our income, we should consider too whether our partners have had to consider exactly the same options, and what choice they did in the end make. I bet you it was in favour of the family, rather than themselves. And to those who ask "what's the point in two people losing out, when it could be just one?" my answer is simple. It pretty much always seems to be the woman who gets the raw deal, doesn't it?

I am, in this, being purposefully provocative and arguing from extremes. Of course every family has its own circumstances and every family will muddle its way through to find a childcare arrangement that works best for them. What I hope to do is to prompt us to think deeper and more creatively about what we should all do with our working lives to ensure men's stated desire to spend more time with our children is actually followed through.

It's all too easy to say, as one guy did to me, "it's just not done in my industry". As if that's the matter dealt with. I'd like to be equal, but it's just not done, so that's the end of that. In our working lives, we need to be able to ask: why isn't it done? And what can I do to make it happen? I don't *really* want men – or women – to sacrifice themselves and their careers on the altar of childcare. I know things aren't as black and white as that. I'd just like to see men particularly, but women too, consider the opportunity of a fairer parenting arrangement more seriously. For the conversation to start not from *it'll never work* or *it's just not done*, or not considering it at all, but from *what might we do to make it work?*

If anything, it's a call for more effort and creativity. Men are well overdue a grown-up conversation about what we really can and should be doing with our working lives, and how we can balance that with our childcare responsibilities. The new fatherhood myth falsely claims that the conversation is already done and dusted. With recession, changing working patterns, the rapid gallop of new technologies and progressive attitudes to gender roles developing at pace, now is as good a time as ever to get that conversation going for real, and to take action ourselves. Because with a bit of creative thought, and a lot of juggling, a fairer partnership in work and childcare is possible, even despite the age-old role models, legislation and attitudes.

9

Doing the sums

AS WE'VE SEEN, men's reluctance to swap working hours for childcare time may be partly down to the difficult issue of family finances – making money and childrearing work together effectively. Concerns about cash do seem to be the most often cited reason for men to stay at work, rather than work part-time or flexibly. There's no doubt that money is a significant worry for all families, but particularly those on lower incomes, and that's bound to play a significant role in decisions about all aspects of childcare: who goes out to work, whether to use nurseries and childminders, and however else the childcare cake is cut.

For some families splitting childcare more fairly between the mother and father will never even occur to them. It's just the way things are: men's roles and women's roles. For a significant number of other families though, couples will have 'done the sums'. This is the most frequently used argument among my own friends about why a more equal share of parenting during the working day isn't possible. But here's a strange thing: pretty much every one of my peers, men and women, are university educated, and are or were in professional jobs before children. Their wives or husbands too are pretty much of the same class and educational background. Yet in every case, it is the man who 'the sums' have dictated should go back to work.

It's a pattern that's repeated across the country: in middle-class, professional couples, it is largely the man who goes to work, and the woman who stays at home or works part-time, even if they were both pretty much on a par career-wise before baby came along. Now, I'm not so rude as to ask my friends what they earn. But an estimate reveals that – before children came along – the blokes and women in about two-thirds of cases must have been earning around the same. In some, the woman definitely came out on top. In some others, the woman often appeared to have already chosen a lower-status, lower-paid job on the presumption that pretty soon they'd be having kids anyway.

In a couple of cases, where both men and women were self-employed and their earning potential and working hours were hugely variable depending on what work they did, it was still the man who continued his work. In another couple I know, the man who worked full-time became disillusioned with his job, and decided to chuck it all in. Instead of taking over a share from his partner who already worked part-time to fit in childcare, he decided to go off and do a full-time second degree instead – for which he, of course, was not being paid at all.

Are we really to believe that even by their late twenties the pay gap between childless men and women is already so huge that it really leaves couples with no choice? In fact, the opposite is the case. Women's full-time hourly pay is actually slightly higher than men's in the 22-29 age group (a pay gap of 3% in favour of women), that being the age when most professional women are building their careers.[1] Look again when employees have reached the 40-49 age group – that is, after children have come along. Suddenly the full-time gender pay gap has taken a radical turn in favour of men, sitting at 15% in favour of men in their forties, and 18% in favour of men in their fifties.[2] And indications are that while the closing of the pay gap is progressing, the rate is slowing down.[3]

Women's tendency to go off and be primary childcarer is what *causes* her pay and promotional opportunities to be restricted, not the other way around. Though it can become a self-fulfilling prophecy: women know they'll get paid less later on, so they decide to become the primary childcarer.

And by the way, until 2011 girls routinely outstripped boys in the number of A and A★ grades achieved at A-level. Women school-leavers are 30% more likely to apply for university places than male school-leavers. Proportionately, women undergraduates achieve more first- or upper-second-class degrees than men.[4] It's not education or access to the workplace that is holding women back, it's childcare. In 2004, the Equal Opportunities Commission reported that unequal sharing of caring work between the sexes was "the largest single driver of the gender pay gap".[5] Nothing has changed since.

Women find, particularly if they are on extended maternity leave or the boss suspects they may selfishly want another baby sometime in the future, that they are passed over for promotion and extra responsibilities, with all the commensurate pay increases those opportunities would have brought. So instead it is men that get the promotion and extra responsibilities, and the extra pay. The result is that women feature in far fewer numbers among senior management staff, on company boards, as company owners, as chief executives and all the rest of it.

If having a baby didn't necessarily mean a woman was going to disappear from the workplace for up to a year, or if she were to come back for more days a week, and more quickly, perhaps this pay and promotional gap wouldn't be nearly as wide. But that would necessarily entail men making up more of the childcare, and therefore taking a bigger hit themselves in those opportunities. Or to put it another way: men might have to compete on a level playing field with women.

There's another difficult and perhaps controversial issue at stake in the *doing the sums* argument. It's the question of how much is enough? When couples do the sums, do they ask whether between them they will earn *enough* to pay the mortgage, feed and clothe the family, and live a relatively comfortable life by their own standards? Or do they ask which arrangement will end up with the family earning the *most* it can?

There's a subtle but important difference. A fairer share of the childcare might end up with the family earning *enough*, sufficient for the family's needs, but it might not be the most *profitable* arrangement. In his book *How Not To F**k Them Up*, Oliver James – a staunch opponent of nursery care – makes a similar case. Parents put their children in nursery so they can go out to work, he argues, because they want to earn *the most* money they can.

The issue, for him, is so important that he argues that if you can't make ends meet without putting your child in nursery, it's not the child that should suffer, but you: reduce your outgoings, slim down your holidays, eat out less, get a smaller house and a smaller car. Making those sacrifices, he says, are better than packing junior off to nursery every day.

I pass no comment on his conclusions about nurseries, but in our own attitudes to doing the sums over childcare, is there not a similar question about where our limits and values lie? Some will be convinced that a more equal parenting relationship, including during working hours, is so valuable and important for their children that they're willing to simply earn *enough* between mum and dad's jobs to allow that to happen. Others will believe being able to earn *more*, even if it means an unfair parenting relationship, works for them because it means the child benefits from a bigger house, more holidays, more toys and gifts, or possibly even a private education. It is up to all of us where those priorities lie, but let's at least go into it with our eyes open. That way, when we do the sums, every part of the equation gets a fair hearing. I wonder how many of us have seriously considered this issue at all?

Meanwhile, those who are influenced by the financial numbers alone might be overlooking that the tax and benefits system actually favours two parents working part-time (or earning lower salaries) over one parent working full-time (and earning a big salary while their partner earns little). Two parents earning below the higher-rate tax threshold will earn more take-home pay between them than if just one parent was on that equivalent salary by themselves.[6] Meantime, if both parents earn less than £50,000 a year, HMRC won't claw back any child benefit, whereas if one partner earns more than £50,000 they'll lose child benefit (on a sliding scale) whether the other partner works or not.

But when it comes to doing the sums, there's yet another aspect missing; another argument I hear all the time. She *wants* to stay at home and look after the children. The woman would *prefer* to be with the kids than go back to work, so surely by being the breadwinner men are releasing women to do what they *really* want.

This comes very close to the idea that women are more naturally suited to childcare. It's very rare that we will hear a man claim, and much less act upon, an actual *desire* to chuck in work and become a full- or part-time childcarer. We say we'd like to, but unlike women, we don't actually do anything about it.

For a start, we can't dismiss the deeply ingrained social stereotype that looking after children is what women are *supposed to do*, and that any woman who tries to balance or even prioritise work is trying to have it both ways, being selfish, or even acting unnaturally. And on the flip side, men are *supposed* to look after their family financially, by going out to work and earning a good wage – and that societal pressure obviously plays its own role in influencing what we do. In the end we all make very stereotypical choices because we are so influenced by the cultural expectations around us.

But I can't help thinking there's also something else about this doing the sums conversation too; something which takes place even before a baby is born. A couple decides that the woman will stay at home before the man or woman even know what childcare will really entail. Before we had children, we had no real idea about how hard childcare could be, and we certainly didn't realise our careers would turn out to be as curtailed as they were. (Haven't all people with children heard parents-to-be regaling us with their plans to carry on life pretty much as normal, only to secretly think: *you just wait folks, you just wait?*). Do couples sign up to an arrangement they believe to be a fair swap at the start, to find that by the time it becomes clear it isn't, those roles have become so entrenched it's too difficult to reverse?

What woman would want to go back to work knowing her status at the office has suddenly reduced, and that her colleagues will raise their eyebrows every time she has to go and do the school run? Who would go back to work in the knowledge their pay grade and promotion opportunities are forever restricted, and they can only go back part-time anyway, and even then there's half-term, Easter, Christmas and the long summer holidays to worry about? Staying at home quickly becomes more favourable. And anyway kids are also really lovely and cute, and the woman has – because she's the one who's put in all the long hours – developed a really strong bond with her child that she'd be reluctant to break.

So women end up staying at home, or in insecure, low-paid jobs, while men enjoy more pay and career security. It's a habit, established even before the baby is born, that's very difficult to break. For women, work becomes something they do between childcare. For men, childcare is something they do – or say they would like to do – when work doesn't get in the way. When times get tough, women and men retreat to their entrenched positions. Men work longer hours to meet the bills, while women do more of the childcare that allows men to do the long hours.

Of course some women *are* born childcarers, and they like nothing more than to spend their every waking hour with their children. But there aren't as many as we'd like to imagine, and surely there are men too who are just as *born to* do large heaps of daddy daycare. And perhaps more men might discover they were, if only they would try it.

But because some women are good and natural and want to do it, that doesn't mean all women are or should be the first port of call. And it doesn't mean that they're bound to absolutely love it and not regret giving up their career, once the baby has actually come along. Maybe that needs to be factored in when couples do the sums before the baby is born.

And there is one final point about the woman who says she'd prefer to do childcare at home than go to horrible old work, with all its stresses, gossip, office politics and commuting. Tough luck!

Men have to go out and endure the supposedly hard-working world, and sacrifice the time with our children which we so desperately state that we'd like to have. On that rationality, aren't women actually preventing us from reaching our potential as parents, and our children from benefiting from having dad around more, by selfishly demanding to stay at home? If men should sacrifice some of their working life on behalf of their children, then perhaps those women should sacrifice some of their (apparent) comfort too. Shouldn't women get out of the house, and go and earn a crust so that men get a chance to be with the kids from time to time?

★   ★   ★

No one likes to live their lives according to some big risk assessment. But perhaps when couples do the sums about who's going to work and who's going to stay at home, we often leave ourselves unexpectedly vulnerable. The story most often goes that it is the man who will work full-time because he'll earn the most money. Meanwhile, the woman will not work at all, or will work part-time and earn significantly less. This tends to leave the whole family dependent on the security of the father's job.

One guy I know works in heavy industry. When his baby came along the couple did the sums and decided since he was in a relatively high-paid job (so was she, but anyway) he would continue to work, while she dropped out of work for the best part of a year, then worked part-time after that.

Except that about 18 months into this arrangement, he was made redundant. Because of the mother's employment gap and her need to work part-time, she couldn't earn anything like the salary she once did. And anyway, who would take her on full-time again if she was likely to go and have another child soon, or might give up her job when her partner had found a new one? She'd hit the same glass ceiling in her company that most mothers bump up against. Meanwhile he didn't have the knowledge or self-confidence (let alone the desire) to go from zero to full-time childcarer at home. He ended up working nights, seeing his daughter even less than before, while his wife did even more of the childcare. The comfortable sums the couple had done before the baby came along suddenly didn't add up nearly so well.

The tendency for women to drop out of the workforce completely or to drastically reduce their hours, or to change to less professional jobs on the assumption that their partner's work is secure, can lead in times of recession to some pretty vulnerable arrangements. And this is playing out particularly among middle-class, educated workers. Among my own friends, a handful have been made redundant in this way, leading at the very least to weeks of worry and a scramble to keep up the mortgage repayments.

The man-as-breadwinner arrangement can also leave both men and women in trouble if relationships break down. In worst cases, women may feel they have no choice but to stay in an unhappy or even abusive relationship because they have no other source of income. In others, where parents do separate, women and children (or men and children, for that matter) can be left with little money, negotiating a complex and ungenerous benefits system, as well as the family courts system if there is dispute about custody.

On the flip side, men who don't spend much time with their children because they're always at work – even if they're generously working every hour to bring home the bacon for their family – tend to be given less favourable treatment in the family courts system. Fathers get a more favourable hearing if they can prove a track record of time, engagement and confidence in bringing up their young children. Indeed, if a man isn't registered as the father on their child's birth certificate – and an estimated 50,000 births are registered every year with no father named – they can find themselves disadvantaged when it comes to custody battles in the family courts. The family courts system is perhaps at fault, but men are doing themselves no favours by excusing themselves from childcare in those early years. Worth noting too that where the father is actively involved in his child's upbringing from the start, couples are significantly less likely to separate anyway.

Suddenly, delegating the children's upbringing to mum, while the man works all hours to give the whole family a great life, doesn't seem such a good plan after all. Even if the man's intention is entirely altruistic. We think we're doing the best for our families by earning the big bucks, but we might actually be doing them harm. It turns out that sharing childcare has more on its side of the equation than many couples first consider. When both parents work part-time and flexibly, both the woman and man are able to keep their hand in at work, and both can adjust their working hours and patterns with the demands of their company, the economy, the obligations of childcare, and personal preference.

Work becomes just another significant, but equal, part of the ebb and flow of family life, rather than the man's main role, inflexibly set in stone. The world of employment is already moving towards a bias for part-time working, shifts and contracts. The time could be ripe for men and women to work out a more flexible and equal working-childcare arrangement between themselves, benefiting our children and our family's financial security into the bargain. And the more we demand such working patterns, the more employers will feel compelled to offer them. But we do have to demand them.

The problem is, of course, that many fathers of young children are already locked into a full-time working life, while their wives and partners are locked – willingly or not – into being primary carer, perhaps working part-time. And it is very much more difficult to break that arrangement, once it's already set up.

We are given the best part of nine months' warning before a baby comes along, more if it takes us a bit of time to conceive. In that time the woman plans all kinds of acrobatic ways to balance her career and childcare. Yet men aren't even attempting the same. The presumption is that they'll simply carry on as they were. Once baby comes, the whole family becomes locked into a working arrangement that is almost impossible to change, even if we later regret it.

It's another good reason why men's active involvement with children should begin even before the baby is born, with the man as well as the woman attempting to change their working patterns towards a fairer share of the childcare. And a fairer share of going out to work. It would not only lead to happier, more confident babies, as well as more secure marriages and partnerships. It would create a more balanced and flexible working arrangement between couples that can better deal with the peaks and troughs of work and the economy.

10

Flexible fatherhood

SO WHAT HOPE for more flexible and part-time working for men as a real and realistic solution to the childcare conundrum?

Women have found that working part-time or flexibly is not only a convenient way to mix home and work, but absolutely necessary. Childcare is expensive, so working full-time for mothers infrequently pays its way. Better to work reduced hours, so that costly child carers, nannies and nurseries can be kept to a minimum. Much better for women to ask for and use flexible working arrangements, so that the school run, illness, half-term, holidays and teacher-training days can be more easily accommodated.

It's no surprise that the newspapers talk of women *juggling* home and work, because that's exactly what they do. Where women do work, they're forced to constantly keep the childcare and employment balls in the air at the same time, often resorting to intricate and ingenious swapping arrangements with other mums to make sure everything doesn't come tumbling down. At the pre-school gates, I've lost track of which mum belongs with which kid because groups of women so often swap the school drop-off between them so they can get to work on time. Shouldn't more men be catching at least some of these balls, at least some of the time? The juggling wouldn't be nearly as much of a struggle if men routinely worked part-time or flexibly too.

But they don't. A working father generally means a father who works full-time, whereas a working mother means a mother who works part-time. A mother who works full-time, meanwhile, is selfishly trying to 'have it all'. Far from changing their working patterns or reducing their working hours when children come along, men with children actually work longer hours than those who don't.[1] Working men may say they wish they could spend more time with their children, but they don't actually back that up by working part-time or flexibly in order to do so.

Just 6% of the workforce are part-time men, compared with 21% of the workforce that are part-time women. While a full 45% of the workforce are men working full-time, and 28% are full-time working women.[2]

When children come into the equation, the differences are even more stark. Two-thirds of women with children are in work, but women without children are far more likely to have jobs. When their children are under five, just under half of women don't work at all. Meanwhile, men with children are actually *less* likely to work part-time than men without children. Just four in every 100 fathers work part-time.[3]

Part of the problem rests with employers who are reluctant to change their old-fashioned working practices, and let men work part-time. Fathers are more likely to have requests for flexible working turned down than mothers.[4]

But cementing that old-fashioned stance in place is that men simply aren't asking to change their working practices. A couple of fathers who do long hours have told me privately that one of the main reasons they stay late so often is exactly to avoid the tea-, bath- and bedtime chaos. Go home early? You must be joking.

Mothers with young children are three-and-a-half times more likely to make flexible work requests than men are.[5] Of the half of working fathers who said flexible working was available to them, only three in ten were actually taking up the opportunity.[6] (In fact, men were more likely to ask for flexible working for non-childcare-related reasons, like study.)

In a Department for Business, Innovation and Skills survey on work-life balance, men didn't rate flexible working as much of a priority when choosing a job. Two-thirds of fathers rated it as not important. Half of women thought it was very important, while only 16% of men did.[7] Around a third of mothers regularly use flexible working, compared with only one in five fathers. Nearly one in ten women use flexible working to accommodate school and pre-school term times, while only one in 100 men does the same.[8]

Some men say they're too scared to ask for changed working practices because they'd be regarded as not committed to their jobs, or that it would affect their chances of promotion. And it's true: what better evidence than the fact that this is exactly what working women experience when they have children? The reality is that it's not easy for men to work part-time or flexibly, particularly if their wives have already reduced their hours or aren't working at all. The sums just wouldn't add up, even if they did ask for and were granted part-time working.

The point I'm making is that we continue to construct

our lives so that this challenge exists, and it doesn't have to. In a world where men are paid around the same as women before children come along, why is it almost always the woman who goes part-time or flexible? Why aren't I writing here about women dropping their hours, so men's opportunities are not curtailed?

Of course there are some jobs that just are not amenable to part-time working. That doesn't detract from my main argument that it's always the bloke doing these necessarily full-time roles. I'm not talking about men's sacrifice for its own sake, I'm talking about a move towards a fairer deal for all working parents, whatever their gender. Instead of treading the same old path, shouldn't the future of our working lives be something more akin, where it *is* possible, to what journalist Gaby Hinsliff, a member of the government's Family Friendly Working Hours Taskforce, calls a 'swinging door' approach. That is where both parents work two or three days a week, but not at the same time.

In our own working lives, my wife and I have forged flexible working patterns that benefit ourselves, our children and our employers (which in my case means me). It's hardly romantic, but Sarah and I maintain a shared online calendar where we can see each other's work commitments, so can plan our own around those things already in the diary. We both enjoy a mix of working at home and commuting for meetings and project working: for her, that can include flights to Belfast from Essex, far more than the average commuter has to put up with.

Every fortnight or so, we'll sit down for twenty minutes to iron out any conflicts: what meetings can be moved, who's going to do the school pick-up on that day, and who most needs or wants to work on a Friday afternoon anyway? A handful of the extra days I'm spending writing this book, I'm *borrowing* against extra childcare days I'll do in exchange when it's finished. In the summer, Sarah spent days in Spain and Norway chasing stories, which she *repaid* to me in childcare when she'd returned. And it works. We get our work done (in fact, we get far more done than if we had to traipse into a soulless brick building every day); our employers – I can be very tough on myself you know – are pretty happy; and our children are well looked after, without the need for formal childcare which we didn't want.

Others will have different solutions to ours. Flexible and part-time working by definition can be as broad as the employer and employee can determine between themselves: squeezing five days into four; working weekends; splitting the day up into three chunks, rather than two; results- or project-based workloads, rather than ones based on hours present at work; time-banking; one week working, one week off; whatever works for you.

The weak position is for men to dismiss part-time and flexibility because 'it'll never work', or 'the boss wouldn't allow it', without even asking, considering it or trying to make it work. We're paid by our employers to find solutions, project manage, negotiate and compromise in our working lives, yet we sometimes apply none of those skills to our own relationships with our employers. Just because our employers don't currently offer such arrangements doesn't mean we shouldn't ask for them, or pursue such opportunities when taking on new jobs in the future.

We may not realise it, but men have exactly the same right to ask for flexible working or reduced working hours to look after children as women do, and employers are legally obliged to consider those requests.[9] In fact, from 2015 all workers will be allowed to ask for flexible working for *any* reason.

Bosses can only turn us down – whether you are a man or a woman – for 'sound business reasons', such as the extra cost, their inability to meet customer demand, or their inability to recruit replacement staff. That may still leave employers with a pretty broad scope, but they can't just dismiss your request without giving it some thought. They have to give a formal written justification for why it is being refused in your specific case, which you can of course challenge. Interestingly, inconvenience and extra cost alone are not usually sufficient justification to say 'no'.

Your request for flexible working can't be turned down just because you are a man, and nor can your boss make an assumption about your family circumstances – like saying you've got a wife to do that kind of thing, so I don't have to let you work part-time. If they refused a man's application for flexible or part-time working, but granted it to a woman in the same or comparable job, employers would be in very big trouble indeed at an employment tribunal.

Which puts men who want to make their work flexible or part-time to do more childcare in a pretty good position. If our employers are already allowing women of the same grade and position as us to work flexibly or part-time, they simply cannot risk refusing our own request to do the same. Like women, we have to follow specific procedures for asking for part-time and flexible working, and we can only apply once a year, if we want to be covered by employment legislation. And we do have to actually ask.

But it is, of course, unwise and probably not a little impolite to just storm in there during our manager's lunch break, waving a trade union flag and a copy of the Employment Rights Act 1996, section s80F. We're more likely to be successful if we build a sound written case for why we want to change our work situation, and what ideas we have for helping the business to continue to thrive in the new regime, or why the new situation might even be better for the company.

Meanwhile, there is also no difference between men and women when it comes to our right to time off to deal with a family emergency. If your child is sick, gets into a fight at school, has an accident, if their carer doesn't turn up or their nursery is closed thanks to a burst pipe, both mothers and fathers have exactly the same right to take one or two days off – unpaid, though some employers will pay anyway – to care for the children. If you need longer than a couple of days to deal with a problem, both men and women also have exactly the same right to use their allocation of annual leave to do so.[10]

Flexibility, exchange, negotiation and change is surely better than 9-to-5 plus overtime plus commute for the bloke, with a constant juggle between low-paid part-time work and childcare for the woman. In a modern workforce, supported by new technologies, most employees and employers could work out far less rigid approaches to our working hours and even the location of our work. We could be pursuing a working environment where good performance is rated more highly than mere presence, where happy employees with a work-life balance are regarded as contributing to, rather than hindering, a decent bottom line.

It turns out that this is what many progressive and still very successful companies are now pursuing. And they are seeing decent business-focussed results. For some, it was the only way they were able to stay in business during the recent recession.[11]

The Family Friendly Working Hours Taskforce reports that companies that pursue flexible working report falling absenteeism, higher retention (and thus lower recruitment and training costs), increased productivity, better choice of employees from a wider talent pool, and greater loyalty among staff. The more companies that actively embrace part-time working, even at senior level, the better the job market would become for talented men and women who also wanted to do a decent chunk of childcare. There will, of course, need to be a critical mass. If one senior manager finds a good part-time deal in one company, he or she may well end up stuck in that company and not be able to progress because other companies around the industry don't offer a similar deal. The currently slow movement towards positivity about part-time needs to step up a gear if it's going to create change that works for employers and employees alike. The movement needs to be towards creating *both* a pool of people who want to work part-time and a market of valued, well-paid, rewarding part-time jobs for them to do.

If flexible and part-time working practices – a world of 'swinging door' work - became the norm, everyone would benefit. The concrete benefits to men and women with children are clear. Meanwhile, those without children would look forward to reduced commutes, time with spouses and friends, even the ability to do fun things during the working week, that their jobs had always got in the way of. Everyone would benefit except the business dinosaurs which continue to demand the 9-to-5. They would suddenly find themselves unable to recruit or retain decent staff to sit in their blank, soulless offices full of unmotivated men who wish they were somewhere else.

As one Equality and Human Rights Commission report concludes: "The gap is widening between workplaces where flexibility is 'business-as-usual' and those which have seen little change to traditional patterns."[12]

★   ★   ★

It's not fair to always blame the bosses for making a work-childcare balance unworkable for women and men. To my wife's various managers' credit, they did everything they could to keep her on as a producer. In fact, one of Sarah's bosses asked her why didn't she bring her baby into work one day a week, if that meant she could more conveniently mix the two.

The idea of taking your children to work sounds pretty good on paper, but even the slightest attempt at it reveals it as just another of the ludicrous *growing trend* ideas that zeitgeist journalists are fond of.

"Babies in the office: Who's been sleeping on my spreadsheet?" said one July 2012 article in *The Telegraph*.[13] And from an earlier article in *The Guardian* – wait for it – "a growing number of companies are allowing parents – usually mothers – to bring their babies into work."[14]

I remember my own folks taking me to their place of work during half-term, a home improvement business they ran in Wolverhampton. My brother, sister and I would be set up with our own 'office' (which was a large stationery cupboard with no windows) in an industrial unit off Old Heath Road, one of the grimmer ends of a pretty grim town.

We'd be given jobs like stuffing envelopes and counting leaflets which carried with them an end-of-week wage packet of a fiver slipped into an square brown envelope. And we'd be left free to roam the warehouse and build massive dens among thousands of rolls of itchy fibreglass insulation, spending the whole half-term scratching our skin red raw.

But Dad would treat us by taking us to the pub where he did lunchtime business deals, which to me seemed to entail getting members of Dudley borough council as pissed as he was. And we all got to sit in the car outside until he came out smelling of stale booze and fried food. In his own way, and with the help of a couple of packets of scampi fries and three bottles of Vimto, Dad was mixing involved fatherhood and work, 80s style.

However much fun playing in the insulation was for us during those half-term holidays, I'm sure we were absolute hell for the secretaries (have you got any paper I can draw on?) and the hardened Wolverhampton labourers my parents employed. I can remember one of these men *accidentally* throwing away my sister's doll. Looking back on it, the crime must have been his own subtle way to tell us precocious brats we were getting in the way. Which was fair, given this was a busy warehouse where dangerous and potentially toxic substances were frequently driven around on forklift trucks.

I have made two attempts to mix my own business with parenting. In the first, I took my daughter into our London office while she was still very small (and I could still afford a London office) because I had to pick something up. OK, I wanted to show off a bit too. It isn't until you try it that you realise how poorly accommodated the workplace is for children.

It started off well enough, with work colleagues and others with whom we shared our open-plan space coming to coo over my little girl. But when that had worn off – after about two minutes – they went back to their desks and their computers. Then every little noise, every gurgle and every weep from Erin's pushchair seemed to come out far louder than it did at home. And it echoed around the office, making a fair proportion of the office workers reach for headphones and internet radio stations.

When the time came there were, of course, no nappy-change facilities in our office. So I had to lie Erin down in the meeting room we all shared, every minute wondering if the senior guy who ran the whole set-up would stumble in and my presence there changing a crappy nappy on his boardroom table would go down like, well, like a bag of shit.

When Erin's mild weeping turned into full-blown howling, I finally concluded this had been a mistake from the start. Grabbing her stuff, I rushed out of the office with my hand over her mouth as if I was some child abductor. Not clever, and hardly showing off my fatherhood skills as well as I had hoped.

The next time was only slightly more successful. Sarah was away filming, and I had to go to Birmingham for a pitch to do a magazine for a government quango. It had insisted on the full pitch, all suited and booted, with a meeting at a time of their choosing, not our convenience. Our partners in the project demanded I attended the pitch, so I had no choice but to bring my daughter along for the ride. I had arranged to deliver her to my dad at the station, and he'd agreed to come up from Wolves to sit with her in a Bull Ring shopping centre coffee shop while I went off for the pitch. As the train rocked along the West Coast mainline, I tried with my partners to finalise PowerPoint presentations and our killer lines, while Erin was bounced up and down on my knee and kept entertained by my waving Virgin coffee cups and sugar sachets in her face.

"If she starts crying, just buy her a croissant," I urged my old man when we hit New Street Station, to which he incredulously replied: "A croissant? This is the Black Country, son, not that fancy London." Perhaps he'd have preferred to feed her black pudding and half a pint of Banks' Mild, I don't know. But at least I'd solved my childcare problem for an hour or two.

I didn't blame my business partners for thinking my mind was not fully on the job, but we did win the tender in the end. And bless him, my dad abandoned the coffee shop and took Erin to the aquarium to buy her a cuddly fish. Which is kinda sweet. So it all came out good in the wash, but it could have been so much worse.

That day I concluded the same as any sane person does if they try it: the workplace is no place to take any children, at any time. Man or woman, journalist or not, we have to find a way to keep work and our children separate. Whatever the cost.

11

Taking care

I HAVE THIS great idea for solving the whole working-hours versus childcare-hours problem. It's that the guys who are responsible for setting our office working hours – generally the 9am to 5pm that we're expected to be at our desks – and the guys who are responsible for setting the hours for formal childcare and school – generally 9am to late lunch or 3pm – should get together and have a jolly good fist fight.

I'm imagining one of those cartoon scraps in a cloud of dust, Tom and Jerry style; the occasional tie or pair of patent shoes being flung from the melee, followed by the ubiquitous childcarer's apron, some cuddly toys or one of those half-tambourines that my daughter's teacher shakes to tell the children it's quiet time. The fight will be a messy affair but with no real harm done. And what will finally emerge might be a consensus among our employers and the people we pay to look after our children about how the hours that govern our lives might dovetail that little bit more conveniently.

Say for example that school started a little bit earlier and work maybe a bit later? What about childcare going on a bit longer, and the end of the working day being a shade sooner? I don't know. How about something that actually serves better the many millions of the population who have both children and a job, who might find something that links up a bit more seamlessly a little more conducive to sanity?

Anything has to be better than the mad scramble we currently endure, the finely balanced daily juggle we find ourselves attempting that can be all too easily thrown out by one too many red lights on the way to work, or our little girl refusing to get into the car until the currently missing cuddle bear is strapped in with his own seatbelt.

Is it only me that wonders what the hell is the deal with starting the school and working day at exactly the same time? Which Einstein's idea was it to arbitrarily stop school smack bang in the middle of the afternoon, when working parents have barely got back up to speed after their lunch break?

Even teachers, who to a casual observer maintain the same hours as our children, can't make this clash work for them. They have to be in work *before* they drop of their own children at school, and then they continue working for a good half-hour after their own children have finished. I would frequently see one of Erin's pre-school teachers frantically sprinting down the road past me after I'd dropped my daughter off – that'll be my daughter this teacher was supposed to be looking after – because she had had to deliver her own child to a primary school at the other end of town.

By the way, those of us without a knee-jerk reaction to teachers and their apparently easy lives will know that most are expected to do lesson planning, marking and work on their own personal development on top of those apparently shorter and more convenient hours, after they've put their own children to bed, and while we're dozing on the sofa watching *The Great British Bake Off*.

Of course there are wrap-around clubs at many schools now, where teachers or others come early and stay late to teach gardening or *papier mache*, cooped up into one of those cold, damp mobile classrooms that looks like a festival toilet, because the main school building has long since closed. But let's not kid ourselves that this is either real teaching or real childcare. It's a stop-gap to allow us to spend an extra hour at work to earn just a shade more than we have to pay for the privilege of doing so. And there's nothing more depressing for us, or for our children, than picking them up from school at 5.30pm when most of the other children are long since home, and the caretaker is waiting grumpily by the gate to lock up for the night.

Nursery care. School. Nannies. Pre-school. Childminders. These are supposed to offer the great release for working parents. We can go back to work because there are a dozen options for our children's care during the day, and if governments are to be believed, they are key to making family and working life chime in beautiful synchronisation. Good, efficient, cost-effective childcare should release women back to work, improve the economy and leave families happy. Only they don't quite work like that, do they?

I don't know any parent who says: oh yes, it works just great for us. It's cost-effective, the nursery is of quality and it offers exactly the hours we need. I never have to leave work early, or in a rush. It's all quiet, simple and convenient. Instead, all the working parents I know seem to be in a deeply unsatisfactory perpetual struggle to make formal childcare decent, affordable, uncomplicated and even possible. And it's a battle made far worse because it is often the woman who struggles to square the circle alone, while men tend to carry on more or less oblivious with their own full-time, comparably hassle-free working lives.

Let's start with the cost, and here's the general rule: one child in childcare is a pretty sound deal. Women, and it is usually the woman, are released to work more hours, which more than pays for the childcare, and everyone's happy. But two children? Nah, that becomes what politicians call 'prohibitively expensive' and normal people call 'a fucking riot'.

As soon as childcare for two little ones kicks in, it becomes nonsense for the woman to work the restricted hours she has to – because of the little problem of crappy dovetailing as already mentioned – and so she often bails out of work completely to look after the kids.

Of course, the government does pay for all three-year-olds to have 15 hours of free childcare a week, though there's some form filling and rules to abide by. While those hours are a welcome help with the cost of childcare, they don't solve the juggling problem. Someone still has to pick up three-year-olds in the mid-afternoon on a daily basis. Individual, self-employed childcarers too have their own lives, their own families, their own homes, so any childcare done by them – which is more expensive anyway – is still going to be a matter of negotiations, deadlines and muddling through.

And anyway, I know of one couple where the mum works, the man doesn't, and they still employ a full-time live-in nanny to look after the children. If you're the kind of couple that can afford a live-in nanny while the dad doesn't work at all, I suspect many of the issues in this section don't really arise for you anyway.

Is it me, or does part-time childcare like this actually cause more problems than it solves? The woman works the part-time hours she can scratch out between the drop-off and pick-up times, rather than rebuilding a proper career. And then schools, pre-schools and nurseries don't operate – by definition – during the school holidays, and self-employed childcarers selfishly take holidays themselves. So even her scratched out convenience of work and childcare is thrown into disarray every six weeks or so, and for the seemingly unending summer holiday every year. Which, conveniently for the holiday companies, also offers a prime time to hike up the price of everything.

How can a woman rebuild a career, or even see a decent-sized project through, if every half-term, Easter, Christmas and summer, she has to disappear again because school's out? And frankly, what employer is going to be delighted with that state of affairs? Yet it is usually women who are expected to solve the puzzle, to keep all the balls in the air, with no reference to men.

One woman spoke of her full-time husband being un-willing to drop his working hours so she could increase hers. If she wanted to increase her working days, the only option was for their son to go to nursery. And guess who had to traipse around five nurseries to look at the facilities and to try to find a convenient day for their son to go? Well, he couldn't ask for a day off to go looking around playschools, could he?

I've heard tales of men magnanimously saying *he* would pay for the extra nursery hours himself, so his wife could go back to work. Or to put it another way: on his share of the childcare days, he'll pay for someone else to do it rather than do it himself. Very generous, that. As if pulling out a wad of cash is exercising his parental responsibility.

This isn't buying a new sofa we're talking about: *she knows more about making the house look nice, so she can choose it and I'll pay.* Right now men are more likely to sweat over which new car to buy than which nursery to put their children into. If men are going to delegate the hours of childcare we ought to be responsible for, surely we should show at least a passing interest in who will be doing that childcare on our behalf.

With our own children, we tried to get on with formal childcare. We really did. To begin with we put our nine-month-old daughter into a nursery for a couple of days a week. But because Sarah and I wanted to maintain our jobs as they were, it meant putting her in all day on those days, until 6pm. Sometimes we'd pick Erin up from nursery, and she'd be the only one left in her age room. Sometimes they'd lump our baby in with a few of the older kids, and sometimes her carer would dump her in the middle of the room with a toy, while she tidied up the mess around her. And I can't blame the carer. She wasn't going to be paid the extra time for tidying up once we'd collected Erin, and she certainly wasn't being paid enough to do one-on-one babycare for our daughter.

And anyway, if Erin was sick, or if we needed to swap our working days because of meetings, we still had to pay for those days. It became a pretty expensive way to get the job of childcare done. That's aside from the holidays and training, where the nursery wasn't even open and we had to fudge our work on those days too.

Even that was better than another nursery we visited which put all babies into a line of eight bouncy chairs when they arrived each day, and they were still in those bouncy chairs a full hour later – I went back to check – with the carer reading an adult book to herself, as if she were some kind of zoo keeper, rather than a childcare professional.

Would we men honestly rather have that kind of childcare, than do a fairer share of childcare ourselves?

After we'd moved house, the next nursery we put Erin in was much better and – glory – there was even a very friendly and flamboyant male nursery assistant running her age group. That pleased me in particular because I wanted Erin to see men and women could look after even the smallest babies. And I was disappointed, and not a little surprised, when he eventually left for a new job after getting married *to a woman*.

But even in the new nursery, the old challenges remained. The rush to take Erin and pick her up. The cost mounting up even on days when she was sick or it wasn't convenient for her to go. The fact that Sarah or I didn't really get a decent day's worth of work done on the days we had to do the nursery run, which was the main reason we put her in nursery in the first place. When Reid arrived, along with having read one too many books on the damage that nursery might do to our children, we decided that putting them both into formal care would be too costly.

I have no strong opinion on whether parents should put their kids into nursery or childcare in response to the working hours problem. But let's not pretend it is the full, or even close to full, solution to the childcare predicament. Those kids still need to be taken and picked up, days off and holidays still have to be accommodated, and the general inconvenience of being part of the school and nursery community – paying bills, filling forms, attending meetings, going on school trips – still has to be accommodated, and usually in working hours. And those issues remain a problem for women, more than men.

We are stuck in a situation where women either have to give up their careers entirely and become full-time homemakers and childcarers, or they have to live a kind of work-childcare limbo where they're neither one nor the other. As well as seeing their promotion opportunities and pay limited because they can't give 100% to their employers, women have to suffer more subtle pressures among colleagues when they have to leave a meeting mid-way to do the nursery pick-up, or leave their open-plan office at 2.30pm while their childless women and with-or-without child male colleagues remain behind doing the 'real' work. And men suffer none of this. Because, for them, these are the very excuses they successfully use not to have to do childcare or the school pick-up at all: I can't do it because I have meetings, and if one runs over I wouldn't be able to leave the room. Everyone at work with will think I'm a part-timer, or that I'm not giving as much as they are to the business. I might not get that promotion, if the boss thinks I'm scurrying off to the school run half the week. Women get on with it, while men get away with it.

No working parent I know is happy with the childcare solution they have. They're in constant search for something that works better, but nothing ever turns up. Our working lives just aren't constructed to seamlessly mix formal childcare and work, something that's made even more difficult because men's time and opportunity to do childcare so often seem to be excluded from the available options.

But wait. Aren't I missing one luscious and seemingly unending stream of free, convenient and flexible childcare, taken up with gusto by many parents as a solution to the work versus childcare imbroglio? Grandparents, please step forward.

According to Grandparents Plus' analysis of the British Social Attitudes Survey, around seven million grandparents now provide childcare for their grandchildren. Nearly one in five grandmothers, and one in eight grandfathers, provides over 10 hours of childcare a week.[1] The baby boomers – our own mums and dads – have become a childcare option that allows us to go off and earn our money.

And what's not to like? Our children get to spend time with people they're familiar with, and who instinctively love them. We don't have to pay them (though some do), and if we're lucky, well, Granny might just run a Hoover round, and Granddad might put up that shelf we've been meaning to get round to. (The insurer RIAS estimates grandparents' contributions save UK parents £11bn in childcare costs over a year, though Grandparents Plus puts that figure at £4bn. Still, quite a sum.)

Of course, not all of us can benefit from this wondrous resource. One of my children's grandparents lives in another country, another can just about go to the toilet by themselves let alone help a child to do so. And as another of the grandparents quite rightly says: the best grandchildren are those you can give back when you've had enough.

But even if they could or wanted to, I'm not sure I'd be that game to let grandparents do the childcare if I found myself too busy working and earning to do it myself. Forgive me for being naïve and socialist about it, but there's something that doesn't quite sit right in the idea of my own folks providing childcare for free, so that I can go out and enrich myself. Even if I was paying them (and I wouldn't be able to use childcare vouchers or the government's 15 hours a week to do that unless they were officially registered, Ofsted-inspected childminders), it would still mix the domestic and financial in rather an uncomfortable way. What next? Dad, can you help me paint the landing for £10 an hour?

I know of one case where grandparents drive 100 miles each way to look after their grandchildren for two days a week without so much as petrol money being refunded. In another ludicrous situation, the grandparents do the childcare for free, so the mum can go to work and earn money as a professional childminder. Note too that grandparents don't earn any legal rights by doing this free work. If couples break up, grandparents don't automatically get to continue their childcare duties or their relationships with our children. In fact, on divorce they have no legal right to see the children at all.

Plus, we all know it's really granny doing the childcare, isn't it? Except in very rare circumstances, our own dads did less of caring for us than we do of our own children. Granddads don't suddenly become all new man when looking after grandchildren. Granddads take the good bits then go for a snooze under *The Telegraph*, while our mums deal with the nappy changes, tantrums, cooking and clearing up. Twice as many grandmothers provide childcare as grandfathers. Which is really a double helping of gender inequality, isn't it? Not only have our mums had to bring us up alone, while our dads went out to work. Now they have to bring up our own kids too. In fact, many younger grandparents are also caring for their own frail parents as well as our kids, Grandparents Plus says. Triple whammy.

Now, don't get me wrong. Lots of grandparents love to be with their grandchildren, and some do actively want to be involved on a weekly basis. But articles in older people's magazines, and materials put out by grandparents' organisations, also show many grandparents are frustrated by their role as first-port-of-call childcarer. Some secretly think it's unfair too, even if they're willing to do it anyway.

Other grandparents are able to make the distinction between occasional childcare so we can go away for a weekend, and regular or even day-in day-out childcare so we can go to work. We shouldn't necessarily accept their willingness to look after our kids as simply the end of the story.

First, it's just not fair that they should miss out on their retirement to essentially go back to work (even if they enjoy it), only this time unpaid. Second, retired grandparents could be doing something more broadly socially useful like working with disabled people, running committees or being magistrates – or as my own in-laws do, by volunteering at a wildlife centre – instead of caring for children three days a week, which can only benefit me and my wife. And third, well, our parents would do anything for us, wouldn't they? That's what parents do. They see us in a struggle, or our desire to further our careers, and they step in to help even if it's not in their interests to do so. That's what being a parent is.

Only, isn't that exactly what we're failing to do for our own children by not putting them before – or at least on a par with – our careers, our earnings, our convenience and our ambitions? And if we're not willing to look after our own kids now, what's the likelihood we'll do it for our own grandchildren when our kids have grown up, and we've grown old?

Grandparents have of course been intimately involved in childcare for generations, but traditionally families lived very close together (if not even in the same house). The care was mutual, with various generations doing a share of the cooking, cleaning, care, support and earning. The very definition of family was different from what it tends to be today, where the family unit is much more likely to be based around two parents with their children, with grandparents brought in as extra hands, rather than part of the family itself.

And there's one more thing that just sits a little un-comfortably in my stomach about this whole grandpar-ents-as-childcarers solution. It's that seven million figure. If there really are seven million grandparents out there doing childcare, then even on the most ludicrously high estimates for fathers, there are far, far more grandparents taking care of children during the working week than dads. If one in five grannies are doing more than 10 hours of childcare a week, that's a total of 1.4 million grannies – over 15 times the total number of stay-at-home dads. On even Aviva's most outlandish figure, nearly twice as many grandmothers are doing regular childcare than even the number of men who *claim* to do most of the childcare themselves.[2] The Future Foundation found that mums were around twice as likely to say that grandparents were 'generally in charge of childcare in the home' than their male partner (while interestingly, dads put their share at four times that of grandparents).[3] No wonder at song time, I'm far more likely to see Granny and Granddad with the children than fathers.

When it comes to childcare, dads are the last in line for the job. And willingly. If women can't do all the childcare, stick the kids in nursery or with a childminder. If that's not convenient or affordable, then our folks can look after them. And if they're selfish enough to be incapable, or unwilling, or dead, and if there's absolutely no other option, well maybe the man might take a day off work a week. But only one.

New fatherhood? My granny's arse!

12

Making work work

SO, I'VE HIGHLIGHTED some of the problems that are preventing men from working less and caring for children more. Now, as the trend goes, I'm supposed to present my menu of solutions.

And in books of this type, they generally go something like this: government should more generously fund maternity and paternity pay; men and women should have stronger rights to time off and part-time work to look after children; women should have a legal right to commensurate salaries and opportunities even if they take time off for childcare; men's jobs and pay should gain the same protection that women's have when they take paternity or even extended paternity leave; employers should face the courts if they won't allow men to drop their hours; and on and on we go. All of which I firmly and wholeheartedly believe.

But I worry about trotting out much of the usual think-tank solutions to the work versus childcare conundrum, mainly because such recommendations are often greeted with a casually indifferent sigh: in a perfect world, yes, but don't you know there's a financial crisis on? At best a consultation is launched among politicians and industry big-wigs who wouldn't know what childcare was about if their full-time nanny waved it in their faces. And of course very little happens. Implementing such measures is likely to be extremely expensive and very complex, and will take years to get right. Such recommendations should happen, and I hope this book contributes to them happening just a little faster, but they're not a panacea.

There's one vital ingredient that I've been highlighting throughout this book, which the think-tanks and books on parental equality have been glossing over for too long. For the societal, legislative and industrial framework to be put in place for men to do more childcare, men themselves have to actually *want* it to be put in place. And men have to prove they want it, by actually doing it.

Five work-related excuses that no longer work:

> *"I don't have boobs" – look up expressing and bottle feeding in the parenting books on your wife's bedside table.*

> *"I'm no good at babies" – nor was the mother, then she tried, then she got better.*

> *"The boss would never allow it" – but you haven't actually, you know, asked, have you?*

> *"None of the other blokes at the office do it" – which is why it's all blokes at your office, isn't it?*

> *"He'll turn out gay" – now you're grasping*
> *at straws.*

Before we talk about changing government policy, or sanctions on employers, or financial incentives for families, men need to demonstrate we really want things to change by doing more with what we already have. The truth is, men aren't asking yet for part-time work. Men aren't asking for flexible working. Men aren't taking the paternity and parental leave they are already legally entitled to.

There is already an enormous amount of wriggle room in our current working environment. Surely we have to fully wriggle in the room we *do* have, before calling for more?

When men are routinely asking for part-time and flexible working, and routinely being turned down; when men are routinely complaining to the media and consumer organisations that their right to a family life is being curtailed because of affordability; when men start leaving their jobs because their employer won't allow them to work part-time; perhaps that is the time to start building a stronger case for government policy to change, or for legal sanctions to be brought. But we're nowhere near that place yet.

Isn't it a little unfair to blame employers for not allowing men to work flexibly or part-time, if men aren't actually asking in the first place? Like with anything in the world of work, employers will consider anything if a sound business case can be made. I would encourage my team to come forward with ideas for developing the business, or changing how we did things, as long as they could build a sound case for doing so. One young father employee approached me with some decent ideas about how we could make his working arrangement work better for his family, and together we found a good place that benefited both of us and our work colleagues too.

Lynn Rattigan, part-timer and deputy chief operating officer at Ernst and Young, said in a *Management Today* article on senior managers and part-time work: "You have to approach it from a business perspective – just because I'm a working mother didn't mean I had a divine right to work reduced hours."

If men want to work fewer hours, or more flexibly, we don't have that divine right either. We too need to demonstrate how it can be made to work for our employers, or at very least how it won't be detrimental to the business. We need to make the case that allowing men and women to work part-time, flexibly and from home will create a happier, more dynamic and satisfied workforce, as well as saving the company hard currency. A man who isn't forever watching the clock, and worrying about getting home for bath time (or the bollocking he's going to get from the wife if he doesn't), is a more satisfied employee. A woman who doesn't feel her career, pay and promotion is restricted by asking for part-time work is going to be a less resentful, and more satisfied, employee.

In my own company, all six of us worked flexibly; sometimes from home, and sometimes from the office. We had a relatively laid-back approach to working hours, particularly start and finish times, and everyone had a right – in fact was expected – to work from home at least two or three days a week. Various team members moved into and out of part-time working as their situations changed. As a father myself, I wanted the flexible arrangements as much as everyone else.

One of my team was based in Edinburgh, 400 miles away from our London office. Another lived on the south coast, a two-hour train journey away. Both would come into the office once a month, at most. They didn't have to uproot and move to London to work for me, they could stay put.

We were all in communication all the time. We used online messaging and video conferencing (in our case Skype), and we'd have team meetings every Friday, and at other times if needed, using telephone conferencing. We had online shared drives where we could collaborate on projects, shared calendars and a shared project management system.

Technology enabled us all to work together efficiently and effectively, to have presence in the team without having to be present. I couldn't give a crap what time my team had lunch breaks, or if they made personal phone calls, or even trips to the shops during working hours. They got their work done, they performed well and were responsive, valuable members of the team. That's what mattered. And here's the most interesting thing of all: I saved an enormous amount of money.

By renting a few hot-desks at our London office, instead of having a single desk for every member of staff all the time, the company saved far more than it cost in software and teleconferencing. And into the bargain, my team worked more efficiently and were able to get their heads down on a project when needed without the usual office disturbances. And all of this collaborative, flexible working was taking place not thanks to the latest iPhone apps, or high-end televideo conference systems. Most of the time we'd just give each other a call on a landline.

I'd like to think of myself as an early adopter of a now strong movement for new technology-fuelled flexible, part-time and home professional working, even in big companies. Telecommunications giant BT reckons it has saved over £500 million in property overheads since 2000 by allowing 86,000 employees to work flexibly, of which 15,000 work from home. And those employees, says BT, are 20% more productive than their office-based colleagues.[1]

BT is, of course, perfectly suited to exploiting new communications technology, so offers an example for other big businesses to follow in how they use technology to make flexible working happen. But technology aside, the company also holds regular fathers' focus groups to make sure their needs are met by working practices.

At the other end of the size scale, with just 32 employees, online marketing company Clock reports its own benefits from flexible working, and other work-life balance benefits, available to its employees, "allowing them to design work around their lives, interests, needs and desires". Performance is regarded as more important than time spent at work. Clock says it has saved money on recruitment and managed to retain valuable knowledge in the company, while also enjoying a low sickness rate.

"If you really trust people and give them space, freedom and guidance, you will be repaid with dedication and enterprise," says Syd Nadim, the company's chief executive.[2]

If we can't get something done in today's society – find our way to the pub, calculate our budgets, find a holiday destination – then you can bet someone has invented an app for it. We're finding new technology solutions to very difficult and challenging aspects of our lives, and a whole swathe of technology solutions for things that really aren't a problem at all. If I'm running out of peanut butter I go to the cupboard with my iPhone, scan the barcode on the jar, and it automatically adds a new jar onto my shopping list, due to be delivered in a couple of days' time.

In a world where my shopping is done without my leaving the kitchen, surely the same principles can be put to use to enable men and women to work more flexibly, with varying hours, and from various locations. Amazing technology already exists for shared working, every business can access it for next to nothing, and the business case for such flexible working arrangements has already been made and won. *Think Fathers: How flexible working for Dads can work for your business*, a paper by the Department for Education, contains dozens of examples of businesses, big and small, that have made it work for them, strategically and financially.

For men who want such an arrangement at our own workplaces, we just need to show how to apply it to our own situation, and build that into our flexible working request. Our bosses might then see it as something benefiting them, rather than something that benefits us only, and in which they will lose out.

In the active fatherhood debate, employers are often called on by campaigners to cough up more cash or to extend paternity leave, so that fathers can be more involved with their babies. Having been on both sides of the argument – an active father, as well as an employer – I know it can't be as simple as employers just throwing more money at the issue.

There were a number of other things I tried to do to encourage engaged active fatherhood. I was pro-actively in favour of part-time employment. I was positive about flexible working for men and women. I was encouraging when employees had to duck out for doctor's appointments, or because a child was sick. But more than anything, I tried to set an example myself. I visibly, even proudly, worked part-time and flexibly, setting the tone for the whole company.

Employers are running scared of new fatherhood, because they think it's going to cost them a heap. And their representatives fight tooth and nail to prevent being forced by government to spend money to allow it to happen. Responding to the Queen's Speech announcement in May

2012 that the government would introduce shared parental leave, Simon Walker, director general of the Institute of Directors, said: "The government should be careful not to use this as an opportunity to increase levels of leave. Sharing the allowance is fine, but putting heavier burdens on business in these tough times would not be a sensible move." [3]

The Confederation of British Industry was also positive about men and women sharing parental leave, but warned against increasing the amount of leave: "We are concerned by proposals to increase the total period of parental leave by another four weeks, given the UK already offers some of the most generous provisions in the world," said Katja Hall, CBI chief policy director.[4] They both got their way, when the government dropped its plans to extend paid paternity week from two weeks to six.

But there's an enormous amount that employers – private, public and charity sector – can do to encourage and allow new fatherhood to happen, without it costing an enormous amount. Nudges in the right direction can have a huge impact, but needn't cost a penny.

In my early 20s I applied for a job as an in-house writer with a trade union. I was asked at the interview if I would consider taking the position as a job share. Rather embarrassed, I had to admit I wasn't quite sure what a job share was. To which my trade union interviewer responded: "To be honest, I don't know what it is either."

The union had a policy, probably grounded in women's working rights, of not rejecting good candidates simply because they didn't want to work full-time. A job share is when there are two or more suitable candidates who both want to work part-time, and they share the job between them. Routinely offering the option of taking positions in this way might help to make fathers (in fact all men and women) feel it's OK to work part-time. It changes the assumption that big, important, high-profile and high-paid jobs always have to be full-time, married-to-the-company jobs. Employers, of course, should choose whoever is best for the job. But at least having job sharing as an option might allow the employer to gain from two different people's skills. Why reject the two best candidates, in favour of the third, because only the third is willing or able to work full-time?

Meanwhile, employees get the chance to enjoy a work-life balance, including active fatherhood, that they're really looking for. Even just having "job share considered for the right candidate" written on job adverts would show that the company cares about its employees, as well as its bottom line. These days that's very appealing to job hunters. In the same way, employers could make much more in their job adverts about the availability, or even encouragement, of flexible working practices. That visible commitment to its employees might just rub off on competing companies too, who could suddenly find the best candidates are being offered what they really want – flexible working or fewer hours – elsewhere.

None of this is new. Feminists have been calling for visible commitments to flexible and part-time working for decades, to provide space for women, and mothers in particular, to remain in the professional workforce. And the result has been family-friendly policies in companies which in most cases really mean 'mother-friendly policies' where men don't get a look in. And some of those policies are still not *very* mother-friendly anyway. Perhaps if those policies and working practices were shaped with the aim not only of encouraging and allowing more women into the workforce, but *also* encouraging and freeing up more men to do more with their young children, they might be more effective for everyone.

Whatever the policies, rules and regulations governing how an employer works, nothing does more to shape our working lives than our very working culture. Many employers still have a culture of presenteeism, where being seen sitting at your desk is apparently valued above getting the job done well. Without costing a penny, companies could begin to change this working culture into something that is more encouraging to men (and women) who wish to, or could more effectively and efficiently, work flexibly or from home or part-time, or a combination of all of these.

An occasional crossing of the boundaries between home and work, where employees are encouraged to talk about their children, celebrate their birthdays, even bring their kids to work one day a year, would also do more to make male employees feel that active fatherhood is OK. How many times has your manager asked how your kids are, by name? Wouldn't it be nice if they did? Many companies already host family days, though some could do more to make them feel less like 'bring 'er indoors and the ankle biters to work, so the blokes can show them off' days.

But surely most effective in changing this working culture would be for senior management themselves to take the lead. For them to be active, involved fathers and mothers themselves, working flexibly and part-time because they want to spend time with their children. Imagine the power of a senior male partner telling his reports: you can't call me on a Wednesday, because that's the day I look after little Jimmy. Wouldn't you feel just that bit more relaxed about asking him for a day off to take your son to the doctors? Or even asking to drop to part-time so you can do more childcare? Meanwhile that boss who never seems to go home, whose secretary is always buying flowers for his wife, presents for the kids, and new shirts for him from M&S, hardly makes us feel it's OK to finish our own work even on-time, let alone go home early or take days off to be with our families.

Much management-effectiveness talk these days concentrates on the power of leadership. Managers, the corporate handbooks state, should visibly illustrate the kind of culture they are trying to encourage among those they lead. It takes only one male manager in a company to be proactive about his commitment to fatherhood for other men to follow. And those early followers are likely to be the managers of the future. That means overarching change in our working culture's attitude to fatherhood could happen very quickly. If we really wanted it to.

There is lively debate about the nature of work right now, into which men's role in a fairer deal of childcare should be built. There's a disruption in the old face-to-face, 9-to-5 way of doing work, thanks mainly to new technology. If men don't jump on board to promote and protect our own and our families' interests in this trend, we could be left behind. It's already too easy for employers to outsource even professional chunks of work to cheaper, overseas workers. We should embrace this revolution as a means to get what parents really need from the workplace, because it's going to happen without us if we don't. For graduates moving into the job market right now, new technology is already central to how they've spent their academic careers, as well as how they communicate for their social life. This is exactly how they'll expect their paid working life to be too. Indeed, they might even reject employers who don't offer these ways of working.

All in all, we need to create a movement where a new father (or a new mother for that matter) becomes exactly the kind of employee that business, charities and public services want. An army of happy, flexible, satisfied workers, rather than a stressed workforce of parents forever juggling and squeezing things in. We have to build a business case for such an army, but then we have to get serious. If companies don't see the light and start making flexible workplaces the norm by themselves, we have to take action and start demanding them.

Our industry and political leaders are happy to argue that companies have to pay extortionate wages, offer massive pensions and company benefits, to recruit and retain the best senior staff. And they argue we should keep taxes low to stop the best business brains from moving abroad. Why not force them to offer decent flexible and part-time positions too? Instead of, or as well as, making the UK a tax haven, why not make it a haven for the world's best business minds who want to work part-time? If industry thought it would lose out on potential efficiency savings and profits because it couldn't recruit the best staff, because those staff wanted to work fewer or non-traditional hours, it wouldn't be long before such flexibility was written into every job description.

When employers make it easier for men to combine their fatherhood role with their work, it leads to better individual health, lower absenteeism and higher job performance.[5] Fathers who work flexibly are more committed to their organisation and show improved psychological wellbeing. And listen up, employers: they get less stressed over lower pay, and have better working relationships.[6]

All of which means women and men have to become excited by the prospect of new ways of working, of doing childcare and work in a non-traditional way. But we have to want this cultural change enough to do something to bring it about. Not to be too Marxist about it all, but our own labour remains an asset we can offer or withdraw to get what we want. So give us the flexible working. Or else.

For all their faults, this is where the coalition government's new family-friendly working policies, due to come into force in 2015, could really make a difference for working couples. It's not that the legislation will influence employers to change their practice, though it may subtly do that too. Rather, it gives women more power than ever to refuse to be the childcarer by default.

Under the new rules, a new mother has to take her first two weeks off work after giving birth, while a man is automatically entitled to two weeks' paternity pay. But after that, the couple can decide for themselves who goes back to work, and can chop and change that nine months of parental leave pretty much as they like. In other words, the new rules will take away that admittedly powerful excuse that men have always had to avoid the grind of the baby work: the mother gets paid if she takes time off to be with the infant, while the father doesn't. For the first time, women will have the law behind them should they demand – even before having a baby in the first place – that the father of their child does an equal share of babycare in that first year; that he makes that early career sacrifice, just as she will have to.

The world of work is changing. There is far more part-time work, and far fewer jobs for life. While it seems trite to argue the financial crisis offers an opportunity for working parents, it certainly could provide the impetus for employers and employees alike to reshape the way we work; a reason to seek out a new way of doing things, since the old way doesn't seem to have worked very well. The result will be cost savings and efficiencies for companies, and a fairer deal at home for parents.

13

A man manifesto

AS YOU DO when you're researching any book these days, I turned to the great research assistant in the sky for help and typed the phrase "equal parenting", and various permutations of it, into Google. I was after academic papers on equal parenting in the UK, some statistics perhaps, definitely some first-hand stories of more involved fathers, along with some other persuasive books, articles and papers on men willingly doing a fairer share in the upbringing of their young children. What I found were men in superhero costumes.

First on my search results came Fathers for Equal Rights, an American outfit centred on child-custody battles. Another contender was the Equal Parenting Alliance, all about men's access rights in case of divorce or separation. Families Need Fathers is another such organisation that sprung up in my search, yet another custody-focussed organisation and support group for separated fathers. And of course there was Fathers4Justice: "the campaign for truth, justice and equality in family law" as the site describes itself. These organisations couch much of their work in the language of shared and equal parenting, but it is chiefly concerned with the family courts system, divorce, separation and custody rights, rather than gender roles in child upbringing.

Fathers4Justice, and other permutations of the fathers and fair custody movement, certainly are among the more vociferous on the issue of fathers' relationships with their children. They've quietened down in recent times, but for a good period they managed to commandeer the very idea of 'equal fatherhood' to mean their narrow definition of a father's fair access to children following a relationship breakdown. There was a time in the mid-2000s when politicians and pundits seemingly couldn't move without being trumped in the media by Spiderman clinging to the side of Tower Bridge, or Batman chained to the gates of Buckingham Palace. Whether or not you agree with their tactics, or indeed their very premise, it can't be denied that the guys in silly costumes have put their own definition of equal fatherhood on the political and media agenda. And with mild success. The law may not have changed much in their favour, but our previously comfortable cultural knee-jerk assumption that kids are always better off with their mother, who should control the father's access to them, is not as strong as it once was.

But on the issue of men taking a fairer share of the babycare: on the hard slog of the changing, and feeding, and burping, and cleaning up vomit; on the doing of daycare, the nursery run, the sick days and the doctor's appointments; on attending children's parties, shopping, washing and ironing for their children, and every other aspect of childcare that a really equal father would participate in, most of these noisy voices of men's equality fall strangely silent.

Where is Superman unfurling a 'Full Take-Up of Paternity Leave Now!' banner from the top of Big Ben? Or hurling leaflets at the House of Commons calling for men's legal right to part-time working so they can look after babies? Why aren't Batman and Robin chaining themselves to the doors at the Institute of Directors, demanding a more considered hearing from employers on flexible working? Where are the campaigners hurling balloons of purple powder at politician fathers, demanding they demonstrate equality themselves by doing a fair share of babycare hours – with or without the help of their full-time nanny? Where is Captain America staging sit-ins in department stores because the babychange is always in the bloody women's loo?

For the men in superhero suits, fatherhood equality is all about their rights to see their kids, not their kids' right to a father who does his fair share. The thought that men might have a responsibility to share equally in the upbringing of their babies from even before birth, and thereby possibly earn a clearer right to equal access to them when they're older and more fun, simply doesn't seem to have occurred.

Given that couples who share childcare more equally are actually more likely to have happier marriages and therefore more likely to stay together – and not bring about this whole problem over custody in the first place – it's a wonder that kind of parental equality isn't higher up Superman's agenda. In fact, whenever newspapers print positive articles about men doing childcare, or at least debating the issue of men as childcarers, you can bet that someone will post on the article's online comments section to hijack the discussion and make an entirely different point about 'the real issue' of custody and the family courts system.

To be honest, I don't want the men in stupid costumes as my representatives. But I do want more men to do a

fairer share of childcare and parenting. Which begs the
question: whose responsibility should it be to make equal,
or even just fairer, fatherhood happen? Over recent years,
there have grown up a number of fatherhood organisations
and think-tanks, the largest of these being the Fatherhood
Institute. And it does some very strong and influential
research and lobbying work on the role of fathers: the
barriers that get in the way of them playing a fairer role,
the legislative restrictions, the social pressures and the
institutional prejudices. It also does ever-important work
about fathers and children from deprived backgrounds, in
non-traditional family settings, among separated families.
And it provides training and consultancy for fathers
themselves, and organisations that work – or would like to
work – with fathers. The Institute, and other fatherhood
organisations, keep the issue of fatherhood on the agenda,
providing well-researched information and a well-reasoned,
well-argued case. And their media presence counterbalances
the more super-hero costumed voice of fatherhood on the
TV news shows.

When I began work on this book, I decided I wouldn't
simply repeat the excellent, worthy and important calls made
by fatherhood think-tanks for institutional and legislative
change to make more active fathering a reality. I wholly
support all of them and I can't add much to the debate by
rehearsing their main arguments here. But I think there's
something significant missing from the various fatherhood
campaigns' work. It's that men's own lack of desire to do
childcare, and the lack of social pressure on them to do it,
isn't being properly addressed.

In their rush to lay the blame for inequality and unfairness
only on politicians, on the economy, on societal pressures,
on employers, and on the historical weight of old-fashioned

gender roles, I think men's own responsibility and ability to change their own lives has been drastically downplayed. What's conspicuously missing from the fatherhood organisations, and from other books on shared parenting, is any persuasive argument for why men *should* do an equal or fairer share of childcare. Their desire to do it is simply assumed, and it's not true.

For all the legislative change, and workplace-attitude transformation; for all the releases of social pressure and upturning of traditional gender roles, no change will bring about a fairer share of childcare among men unless men actually *want* it to happen. By campaigning so vociferously for legislative and cultural change, without confronting this fundamental taboo, we're continuing to create the smokescreen of convenient excuses which allows men to get away with not doing their fair share.

We can introduce all the paternity leave we like, but if men won't take it, then it is men that are at fault, not the legislation. We can offer a right to flexible working and part-time hours in every office, but if men choose to stay at work rather than go home, then it's men that need to change, not the workplace. We can provide any number of educational programmes for men on babycare, but if the women in their lives interfere when men try to have a go, then it is women (and the men who happily acquiesce) who are doing it wrong.

I say yes to the flexible working, and the part-time hours, and the extended fully paid paternity leave, and the right to time off for children's sickness, and the compulsory liaison with fathers in maternity services, and fathers' rights to sleep overnight in the labour wards, and much more. I say bring it on. Bring it all on right now, with a cherry on top.

But I also say: come on guys, what the hell are we doing?

If the surveys are to believed, men say they want to spend more time with their children. But right now, they're not. If men really did want to play a more equal role in childcare, they would. Change on a family, political and cultural level would come about incredibly quickly if men decided to make it happen. If we refused to work full-time or only took on part-time jobs; if we only voted for pro-equal-parenting policies; if we lobbied our trade unions to support workplace rights for fathers; if we demanded an equal share of childcare from women; if we refused to be fobbed off as second-rate babysitters by schools, pre-schools and children's services; then you can bet parental equality would suddenly become a whole lot easier.

I can't help wondering that at least some of the campaigning energy spent by think-tanks, and a lot more of the pages written on the subject of equal parenting, might be more effectively used by addressing the key question of how to make men *want* to do this stuff, as well as how to enable them to do it.

As one friend perfectly put it: there's only a mild pull on fathers to play a bigger role – they can still choose to do it or not. What's needed is a push – a burning platform that shows they, their children and their families are in a worse situation if they stay put. Currently, the fatherhood platform isn't on fire. It's all too comfortable, thanks very much. The challenge is to make it a little more uncomfortable. How do we set that platform alight?

To start with, we should show the new fatherhood myth for exactly the sham that it is: an entertaining and heart-warming, but ultimately untrue and unobtainable ideal that is actually preventing men from doing a fairer share of childcare. The new fatherhood picture of perfection sets the bar too high for those of us men who'd like to do childcare, but just aren't as good looking, or effective, or self-confident.

Once the new father myth is soundly confined to the dustbin, the next challenge is to persuade men that childcare is worth doing for its own sake, for the sake of their children, and for their families – and that it should take priority over, or at least be considered equal with, other demands on their time and interests. Men will want to do childcare if they are persuaded it will lead to their kids being safer, the wives being happier, their families more secure, and that they themselves will have a better life. All of these things are soundly grounded in research, but have we really made enough effort to let men in on the secret?

Perhaps men won't take extended paternity leave introduced by the coalition because they haven't been properly told or convinced that they should do it, or how they and their families will benefit. We simply assume men want to take extended leave, before we've convinced them they should.

There's also an element of social pressure that is missing. Academics, politicians, think-tanks and authors are quick to note the significance of hundreds of years of social pressure on men to be the breadwinner and protector of their women and children. They argue that those social expectations are so strong that they prevent men from doing childcare. Yet, we seem reluctant to use the power of social pressure to promote a fairer deal in parenting. We shy away from the notion that, in the early 21st century, it might be a significant and important part of the father's very duty and role – the *job* of being a good dad – to be intimately and actively involved in childcare. We're afraid to construct the social pressure that men should put their babies' care before their work, or their embarrassment, or their sporting interests. We seem unable to say: this, guys, is what being a dad is *all about*.

And by the same token, we're reluctant to press women to demand a fairer deal from the fathers of their children, even if that means they have to leave the kids at home and go out to work themselves. We're afraid to say: that's how good parenthood is *done* these days. If social pressures are as powerful as we claim they are, wouldn't this be a very effective route to getting more men more involved in their young children's lives?

After all, these are our children we're talking about. We'd run into a burning building for our kids, put ourselves between them and an attacker. We'd protect them from rampaging dogs, jump into the freezing sea if they fell in. Maybe we'd even start going to church so they can get into a better school, if that's what it really takes. Yet presented with clear evidence that a father's very active involvement from the very earliest age is best for our children and families, indeed for us too, we consistently and comprehensively reject it as too difficult, or too inconvenient, or too expensive, or too boring, or, well, just not for us.

We're willing to allow women to sacrifice their careers, their social lives, their happiness, their fulfilment, sometimes their sanity, because men 'don't do babies'. And women are acquiescing in the whole unequal caboodle. Every family thinks they have a really good excuse for the father not to do it. I've been hearing these special cases since Erin was a twinkle in my eye, and I've even used some of them myself. But that's what they really are: excuses.

The truth is that any man whose partner is bringing up their young children really has no sound excuse for not doing the same. Particularly among professional middle-class men, we have the ways and means to find a way if we're willing.

Maybe you think you'd be no good at looking after children. Do it anyway.

Maybe the women will be mean to you at playgroup, and not involve you outside the school gates. Do it anyway.

Maybe you think you can't afford to work part-time or take a pay cut. Do it anyway.

Maybe your friends, colleagues and boss will think you're a pansy or that you're not playing for the boys' team. Do it anyway.

Maybe your wife wants to do all the childcare, every hour of the day. Well, you have just as much right to want to do it as she does. So start the negotiations.

Because here's the thing about children. They grow up. We can't go back and re-do the hours we've missed with them while we were at work, or at the football, or asleep in the spare room. We can't repay the responsibility we ought to have had for them, once the opportunity has passed. I'm forever hearing from grannies on the bus: "They grow up so fast, blink and you've missed it."

Millions of men across the UK, and across the world, are consistently, routinely and willingly blinking and missing it. Why? Because we're too lazy, or selfish, or uninventive, or stuck in our ways, or embarrassed, to say: men can do it. I'm going to do it.

We need to be able to show men that taking those first steps towards fairer parenting are not as difficult or painful as they think. Sure, no one wants to stick their head above the parapet. Least of all at work, or in circles of friends where men's and women's roles follow the traditional set-up. But everyone who does childcare knows that it gets easier, once you get used to it.

Men might just be surprised at how willing their employers are to grant them part-time work, if they'd only ask for it. We might feel suddenly warm and satisfied if we demonstrate to the women outside the pre-school gates that we know childcare just as well as they do, if we would only give ourselves a chance to show off a bit.

These are messages that should be more clearly articulated to men, particularly those who are already on the cusp of taking the leap. It is among those men – who already know they'd like to do more, but don't quite know how and haven't quite yet taken the step – that a larger cultural change will find its foundations. If those men who would kinda like to have a go at childcare take a lead, others will quickly follow.

It is the human condition to conform with those we see around us. In our workplaces, in our communities, in our families, we rarely see a man working part-time, or taking a conspicuous interest in his fatherhood responsibility. And because we don't see others doing it, we don't do it ourselves. Imagine if we really did frequently see men on the streets doing childcare, muddling along and doing fine. Not perfectly, but we don't see women doing it perfectly either. Imagine if men in your friendship group, or at work, happily and even proudly worked part-time, because of their responsibilities to their children. Wouldn't it be a lot easier to do the same ourselves?

So how should these men who are already on the cusp get started? For a start, maybe the leap from full-time work to exactly half-and-half is too big to do in one go. (It certainly was for me.) Perhaps going from doing very little childcare, to doing it every other night is too much to stomach. How about starting small, and building from there? How about squeezing a five-day working week into four, and taking sole responsibility for your children on a Friday? How about baby feeding or changing on a strictly take-turns basis? Or even one in three changes, to start with? How about Dad taking over from Mum for an hour every day after work, and being solely responsible without her sticking her nose in? (This is what we did during Sarah's first maternity leave.) How about the man and woman divvy up the jobs, and he becomes solely responsible for the baby-related washing, or preparing mashed foods, or handling all bath times, while she takes on some other commensurate job (or just has a sleep)?

Big change begins with baby steps. And those men who didn't take any responsibility at all for childcare? Well, they would soon become the freaks, wouldn't they?

We need to get to a place where playing a fairer or even equal role in all aspects of childcare and childrearing is a conscious and respected choice for a man, not something foisted upon him by guilt, by women, by legislation or by a hackneyed Hollywood storyline. That doesn't mean men doing more than their fair share, or piling childcare on top of an already hectic work schedule. And it doesn't mean men doing a bigger childcare role only to 'free up' the woman to go back to work. It means men wanting to, enjoying and actively pursuing childcare because to do so is good in itself. If that means work, or even the woman's preferences have to be revised to allow it to happen, then so be it: let's start the negotiations.

Men shouldn't want to do childcare only because it's fairer, or because it releases women from the burden, or because of gender equality, or the pay gap, or because flexible working is actually quite good for employers. They should want to do it because it's a good thing.

This, of course, could be just what our employers (and maybe some women) are afraid of: that once one man does it successfully, everyone will want a piece. But that should encourage, not prevent us from taking the leap. We might start outside our comfort zone, but pretty soon it could become a lot more cosy. As other men join in, it wouldn't feel so lonely out there. And then other blokes who had never even considered playing a more active role might see what we're doing and decide to play along too.

All of a sudden men with young children wouldn't be some freakish exception. They would be – *we would be* – just normal blokes, doing normal things that normal blokes do. Not new fatherhood. Just good fatherhood.

Not new dads. Just good dads.

Epilogue

BY THE TIME this book is published, a strange silence will have descended – in the mornings at least – upon our little bungalow tucked into the Essex countryside.

My little boy Reid will start pre-school for a few days a week, going up to five mornings a week all too soon. My little girl Erin will already be nearly a year into 'big school'. From nine until midday every day the house will suddenly become eerily still. Quiet for the first time in five years. The end of a beginning. I shall welcome it with relief and sadness in equal measure.

Half a decade on from taking up equal childcare, I look back with a mixture of bitterness and regret, happiness and amazement. It hasn't been easy, but it's not been without its rewards.

I look back on my working life with at least some melancholy. I chose to put my children above my work, my company, my ambitions. My wife and I both loved work. It

was what got us up in the morning. That's if we'd gone to
bed at all, so enraptured we might sometimes have been with
our careers. Taking an equal share of childcare was to self-
impose limits on my work and that's nothing but a shame.

I am naturally entrepreneurial. What amazing projects
and profitable initiatives I might have initiated in that
time, I'll never know. Childcare probably saved me from
a pursuing a few hair-brained schemes too. I mourn them
nevertheless. I'm bitter for the loss of my work, the enforced
change in my career. The lack of choice that choosing
childcare imposed.

I don't look back with fondness at the reception I have
received as an involved father out in public over the last
five years from services like maternity wards and health
visitors, nor at the legislation that ought to be making it
easier not harder for men to do what I did. I'm not delighted
with my treatment from playgroups and parents' groups,
nor especially from some mothers who've made it far more
uncomfortable than it needed to be. (Though, I'm sure I've
made their lives uncomfortable in my own way too.) I'm
embarrassed for us all that trying to be a fairer father has
sometimes felt so damn wrong.

I won't miss the sometimes unending boredom. The
public singing of Old MacDonald through gritted teeth in a
singing voice that I don't have. I won't miss the exasperating
15-minute operation that is getting a one-year-old out of
the house, along with nappies, coat, gloves, hat, bottles, wipes,
pushchair, favourite toy and everything else I've probably
forgotten, nor having to pile it all back into the house again
because my toddler has now decided she needs the toilet.

I won't miss standing out in a crowd of women with
babies; the awkwardness of watching women watching me
watch women breastfeed. I won't miss having to explain

what I'm doing with a baby during the day, or justifying my work-life decisions as if they're some defiant anarchistic protest. I won't miss being patted on the head by grannies who tell me what a good job I'm doing, for a man.

Was it all worth it? This is where I'm supposed to say an unequivocal and immediate yes. But I'm not sure. I don't know the measure of the things I've missed, the opportunities lost, the fun that not being an equal parent might have been. So I really can't decide. But I do know some things.

I know that I have a deep, almost Borg-like intuitive relationship with my two children. I know them upside-down, inside-out. I can tell a real cry from a fake one, I know hurt before it hurts. I cannot say whether my relationship with Erin and Reid is deeper than it might have been, or whether it is deeper than for fathers who don't do childcare equally; I'll leave those dads to find out for themselves. What I can say is that I would not give up the natural affinity I feel I have with them without a fight.

I have shared the most amazing times with my children – joys I think I could only have missed if I worked more or hadn't put up with the boring, thankless, messy chunks of time in between. They've made me laugh and weep, proud and embarrassed, worried sick and sick of them. They've amazed me with their intelligence, amused me with their ignorance. For those times alone, I would change a million more nappies.

I've had fun. The juggling of the baby equipment in cafés. The crawling into bed with my little ones after lunch to read stories or play dens. The little tricks I've played on them, the little jokes they think they've played on me. The way they can never find me in hide-and-seek. The way they always hide in the same place. The burned biscuits. The scrawls on the wall. The wees missing the potty and soaking the floor.

The cards they have made me. The exasperated tellings-off I've delivered, only to realise I've been unfair. The hundreds of times they've said I love you.

Outside the school gates, in the park, at the playgroup, I have felt proud to be an equal dad. I've been delighted that I can understand and relate when the women talk about their children, even if excluded from the conversation. I'm secretly proud to have stood out as an equal parent, perhaps in my own way influencing other men and women just the smallest amount.

With my partner, wife and best friend, I think we have found a balance, and a fondness, and a mutual respect, and a trust, that can only have been strengthened by our mutual dedication to trying to do childcare more fairly. We've learned to give each other space to breathe, to become good parents as ourselves as well as in a couple. For that, I would endure a million more sleepless nights.

And I know one more thing about wilfully exchanging half of my working life to be with my children. I know that it has taken me twice as long to write this book as it might otherwise have. No one ever promised having babies would be easy.

★   ★   ★

If there's one thing my wife's TV documentary career has taught me, it's that a decent story should always have a twist in the tale, a 'reveal' as TV journalists call it. So here's mine.

It was Erin's fourth birthday, and a couple of months after Reid's second. We'd celebrated with some close friends by having the usual cake, ice cream and balloons at our house. Feeling guilty for the amount of kiddy cake I'd consumed, I decided to knock out a few virtual miles on my turbo-trainer, a souped-up exercise bike. About 20 minutes into a high-paced ride I had a rather strange mild fit. It forced me off the bike and up against the wall, with me holding onto the bike to stop from dropping to the floor.

It wasn't the first time it had happened.

For a couple of months I'd been having these strange episodes while out cycling, but had put them down to pushing it too hard or an exposed nerve in a broken tooth. This episode, though, felt more serious. It was almost like a stroke, and it was time to get something done about it. The next day I saw my doctor, and within a week I'd had an MRI scan. The following Monday my doctor turned up unannounced at my home.

While my kids ran in and out of the house bringing the doctor leaves from the garden, he stared at his feet and told me I had a brain tumour. A tumour that is inoperable and incurable. Sometime in the nearish future, perhaps in a year, perhaps in five years, possibly even in ten, the tumour will turn malignant. When it does, I'm in deep trouble. I will probably be able to get radiotherapy, possibly even chemotherapy. But the tumour is bound to come back, and when it does it will end my life.

The chances of my seeing Erin and Reid reach their teens are slim. The chances of my filling the car with their crap and dropping them off at university, next to nothing.

For the week following diagnosis, I thought of one thing only: my family. If I was to pass away in the next year or so, I thought, then at least I've spent as much time with my children as I could. I am lucky enough to be able to look back on the last five years as equal childcarer and to know I'd squeezed it for everything it was worth. All the difficult decisions and sacrifices my wife and I had made for a more equal parenting relationship had been worthwhile.

We often think about, love and value our children for what they're going to become in the future. And we often wish their lives away, declaring we can't wait until the terrible twos are over, or for their first day at school. More than ever now, I've learned to love and value them right now for what they already are, the age they are, the stage they're at. Because I might not get to see what they'll become. I'm in reasonable health just now, but the diagnosis has redoubled my determination to make every second with my children and my wife count. Because for me there will come a time when the opportunities will run out.

Some children don't get to see their fathers much at all. Perhaps he's already left for work by the time they get up, and he's late back most nights, or home just in time to read a bedtime story. Perhaps he's working long hours now while they're young, so the family can have a big house, great holidays and more time together once they're older. Perhaps he's skimped on the feeding, the nappy changes, the bathing and the playing, and in turn his relationship with his children isn't quite as deep as it could have been. Perhaps he's thinking he'll put in more time with the kids when they're a bit older, because he feels he'd be much better at hanging with teenagers.

We all walk around in a cocoon. We think the worst could never happen to us. As if we're invincible, just getting on with life as it tick-tick-ticks along. Then suddenly, inevitably, something horrific wakes us from our slumber. A brain tumour diagnosis, the death of a child, a disability, disease, redundancy, fire, a car accident, divorce or separation. And then it's too late.

Perhaps then we wish we'd spent more time with our children, enjoying what we had, while we had it. As Sarah always reminds me when I'm feeling miserable about my tumour: no one ever lies on their deathbed wishing they'd spent more time at the football, or more time at work. They wish they'd spent more time with their loved ones.

Despite the brain cancer that will kill me, it turns out I'm one of the lucky ones.

Acknowledgements

Appreciation is due to a number of people for help making this book happen, though all mistakes and omissions remain my own. Particular thanks for the initial critical reading by Nicki and Mike Hyde-Boughey and for Mike's number-crunching spreadsheety goodness. Thanks to Michele Madden at nfpSynergy for providing statistical brainwork when my brain just wouldn't work that way. The customer service staff at the National Office for Statistics were also incredibly patient and helpful.

I'm very grateful to Duncan Fisher and Barney Jeffries, both highly involved fathers, for reading the book and challenging me to refine some of my arguments. Thanks to Ali Rhodes for encouraging me do it in the first place, and to Ali and my brother Darrius for so much support in other ways too. Thanks to my wife Sarah Mole for reading and commenting on early drafts and for being the perfect parenting partner. To Erin and Reid, I hope parental equality will be just the norm by the time you've grown up, and that you'll read all this as a quaint history of what it used to be like.

Continue the debate at www.mencandoit.co.uk or visit the Facebook page www.facebook.com/mencandoit

Rosie the Riveter

The We Can Do It! poster was originally designed in 1942 by J. Howard Miller for the United States war effort. The poster aimed to boost moral among women while men were off at war. It was only later that the image became synonymous with women's empowerment, showing they could take on traditionally male roles and showing that women can make decisions for themselves.

It was then that the woman in the picture – believed to be 17-year-old factory worker Geraldine Hoff (later Doyle) – became known as Rosie the Riveter. My use of the image is intended as thanks and respect due to the feminist movement, as well as a challenge to men to rise to the roles we've traditionally assumed were women's alone.

The poster has been copied and parodied many times, but I have in good faith attempted to trace the original copyright holder. I have only been able to establish that it rests in the public domain in the United States. If I am mistaken, I would be delighted to properly acknowledge the correct copyright holder in any reprints and on this book's website. For the cover illustration, I'm grateful to the pastiche artist Martin Hargreaves who immediately understood what I was after and who produced an image that was far better than I'd imagined it could be. Thanks to John Chandler for making it work as the cover.

Notes

Introduction: The Babysitter Bites Back

1. A notable exception is Duncan Fisher's self-help focussed book *Baby's Here! Who does what?* (2010, Grandma's Stories)

Chapter 1: The new fatherhood myth

1. Daddy stays at home but mummy has flown the nest, *The Telegraph*, 26 January 2012

2. Role reversal: Number of women who are family's main breadwinner soars as husbands left holding the baby, *Mail Online*, 26 January 2012, http://www.thisismoney.co.uk/money/news/article-2092103/Househusbands-triple-15-years-number-women-familys-main-breadwinner-soars.html (accessed 7 December 2012)

3. Is shared parental leave the best way forward? *The Guardian*, 18 January 2011, http://www.guardian.co.uk/commentisfree/2011/jan/18/shared-parental-leave-nick-clegg (accessed 7 December 2012)

4. Wait till your mother gets home, *The Observer*, 29 January 2012

5. Fatherhood Institute (19 January 2011) *Fathers, mothers, work and family*

6. Firms hold dads back when it comes to family, *BT corporate website*, 14 June 2012, http://www.btplc.com/news/articles/showarticle.cfm?articleid=%7Bc66e1862-1b1c-4bbb-8a3d-20fad960e7b6%7D (accessed 7 December 2012)

7. Equality and Human Rights Commission (2008) *Working Better: Fathers, family and work – contemporary perspectives*

8. Working Families/Lancaster University Management School (2011) *Working and fathers: Combining family life and work*

9. Cited in: Fatherhood Institute (19 January 2011)

10. Stay-at-home dads on the up: one in seven fathers are main childcarers, *The Guardian*, 25 October 2011

11. The rise of the stay-at-home dad: One in seven families now have father as primary carer for children, *Daily Mail*, 25 October 2011

12. Breadwinning wives lead to more househusbands, *The Telegraph*, 25 January 2012

13. FATHERS are the main child carers in one in seven UK homes, *The Sun*, 21 December 2011

14. Stay-at-home fathers 'up 10-fold', *BBC News website*, 6 April 2010, http://news.bbc.co.uk/1/hi/education/8605824.stm (accessed 7 December 2012)

15. Never mind the numbers, what about the social trend?, *BBC – Blogs – College of Journalism website*, 8 April 2010, http://www.bbc.co.uk/blogs/blogcollegeofjournalism/posts/never_mind_the_numbers_what_ab (accessed 11 December 2012)

16. 'Modern Day Father' downs tools for cookbooks and dusters says new survey, *Not On The High Street website*, 12 June 2012, http://www.digitalnewsroom.co.uk/noths/modern-day-father/ (accessed 11 December 2012)

17. *Figures for men:*

In 2002, there were 190,000 men who were classified as 'economically inactive, looking after the family/home'.*(i)* In August–October 2012 there were 220,000*(ii)* – an increase of 30,000 men.

In 2002 there were only 80,000 men not working because they were looking after children (42% of the total); the rest were looking after disabled relatives or similar.*(i)* Assuming that proportion hasn't changed (the ONS no longer separates them out), the number of men looking after children full-time in 2012 will be 92,632. That's a growth of 12,632 men in a decade.

In 2002 only 39,000 of these 80,000 men were at home looking after children under school age.*(i)* Assuming the same proportions today, there are 45,158 men looking after children under school age in 2012. That's 6,158 more men looking after babies and toddlers than there were in 2002.

For the years in between, the figures show a pretty slow but steady growth, albeit a small one in total.

Figures for women:

In 2002, there were 2.199 million women who were classified as 'economically inactive, looking after the family/home'.*(i)* In August–October 2012 there were 2.11 million*(ii)* – a drop of 88,000 women.

In 2002 there were 1.707 million women not working because they were looking after children (78% of the total); the rest were looking after disabled relatives or similar.*(i)* Assuming that proportion hasn't changed, the number of women looking after children full time in 2012 would be 1.639 million. That's a decrease of 68,311 women in a decade.

In 2002, 1.101 million of these 1.707 million women were at home looking after children under school age. *(i)* Assuming the same proportions today, there are 1.057 million women looking after children under school age in 2012. That's drop of 44,060 women looking after babies and toddlers since 2002.

  (i) Office for National Statistics (2002) *The economically inactive who look after the family or home*

  (ii) Office for National Statistics (December 2012) *Table: INAC01 Economic inactivity: reasons*

18. Office for National Statistics (2002)

19. For the record, the 2001 and 2011 national censuses actually show a decrease in the number of men ticking the *'economically inactive - looking after the family/home'* box over the ten year gap. Four thousand fewer men self-identified as looking after the family/home in the 2011 census. However, the census allows participants to tick any number of boxes for economic inactivity at the same time, rather than asking for a primary reason for not working as the quarterly ONS's economic activity survey does. The usually vociferous stay-at-home father growing trend journalists seem to have stayed pretty quiet about this particular census result.

20. Office for National Statistics, *Annual Survey of Hours and Earnings,* http://www.ons.gov.uk/ons/rel/ashe/annual-survey-of-hours-and-earnings/index.html (accessed 11 December 2012)

21. Office for National Statistics (2004) *Annual Survey of Hours and Earnings, 2001 Results,* All Employees 1.1a Weekly Pay – Gross 2001

    Number of jobs (in '000s): 21,858
    Male full-time: 10,433 (47.73%)
    Female full-time: 6,160 (28.18%)
    Male part-time: 894 (4.09%)
    Female part-time: 4,372 (20.00%)

22. Office for National Statistics (November 2012) *Statistical Bulletin: 2012 Annual Survey of Hours and Earnings*

23. Office for National Statistics (2006) *Time Use, 2005 Edition,* table 3.1

24. Office for National Statistics (2006) *Time Use, 2005 Edition,* figure 4.4

Chapter 2: Fathers not visitors

1. Royal College of Midwives (2010) *Reaching Out: Involving Fathers in Maternity Care*

2. Various benefits of fathers attending births cited in: Royal College of Midwives (2010); FI Research Summary (20 March 2007) *Fathers attending births*; Fatherhood Institute (2010) *The Dad Deficit*.

3. Are new dads being left out?, *Mother and Baby website*, http://www.askamum.co.uk/Family/Search-Results/Being-a-dad/Are-new-dads-being-left-out (accessed 11 December 2012)

4. Royal College of Midwives (2011) *Research and Development Action Plan 2011*

5. Fathers at birth and beyond, *Midwives magazine*, 19 July 2012

6. Care Quality Commission (2010) *Maternity services survey 2010*

7. New mothers will rate midwives and doctors on childbirth care, *The Observer,* 29 December 2012

8. Scottish Health Council (2011) *Good Practice in Service User Involvement in Maternity Services – Involving women to improve their care*

9. TNS System Three (2005) *NHS Maternity Services Quantitative Research*

10. Fatherhood Institute (2011) *Family Man: British Fathers' Journey to the Centre of the Kitchen*

11. Burgess, A. & Ruxton, S. (2006) *Men and their children: Proposals for public policy,* IPPR

12. National Perinatal Epidemiology Unit (2010) *Delivered with care: a national survey of women's experience of maternity care 2010*

Chapter 3: Why fairer parenting?

1. Cited in: Fatherhood Institute (2010) *Fathers' impact on their children's learning*

2. Flouri, E. (2005) *Fathering and Child Outcomes,* Wiley & Sons

3. Cited in: Fatherhood Institute (19 January 2011) *Fathers, mothers, work and family*

4. Cited in: Civitas (2001) *How do fathers fit in?*

5. Cited in: Fatherhood Institute (2010) *Supporting Families and Relationships through Parental Leave*

6. Cited in: Fatherhood Institute (2010) *Supporting Families and Relationships through Parental Leave*

7. Cited in: National Childbirth Trust (2009) *Involving Fathers in Maternity Care*

8. Cited in: Fatherhood Institute (2010) *Fathers and postnatal depression*

9. Burgess, A. (1997) *Fatherhood reclaimed: the making of the modern father*, Vermilion

10. Cited in: Fatherhood Institute (2010) *Supporting Families and Relationships through Parental Leave*

11. Equality and Human Rights Commission (2009) *Meeting the changing needs of families, workers and employees in the 21st century*

12. Cited in: Fatherhood Institute (2010) *Supporting Families and Relationships through Parental Leave*

13. Cited in: Fatherhood Institute (19 January 2011) *Fathers, mothers, work and family*

14. Office for National Statistics (2010) *Labour Market and Family Status of People, and Women with Dependent Children*

15. Warren, T. (2003) *Class- and Gender-based Working Time? Time Poverty and the Division of Domestic Labour*, Sociology

16. Office for National Statistics (2011) *2012 Annual Survey of Hours and Earnings*, table 6.12a, tab: part-time

17. Beal, N. and McGuire, J. (1982) *Fathers: Psychological Perspectives*, Junction Books

18. Cited in: Civitas (2001) *How Do Fathers Fit In?*

19. Equal Opportunities Commission (2005) *Time Use and Childcare*

20. NHS Health and Social Care Information Centre (2012) *Infant Feeding Survey 2010: Summary*

Chapter 4: 'Doing babies'

1. NHS Health and Social Care Information Centre (2012) *Infant Feeding Survey 2010: Summary*

2. One in ten new parents sleep apart after their baby is born, *Mail Online*, 14 May 2011, http://www.dailymail.co.uk/health/article-1386998/One-new-parents-sleep-baby-born.html (accessed 11 December 2011)

3. Cited in: Royal College of Midwives (2011) *Reaching Out: Involving Fathers in Maternity Care*

4. Lewis, C. and Warin, J. (2001) *What Good Are Dads?*, Fathers Direct

5. National Perinatal Epidemiology Unit (2010) *Delivered with care: a national survey of women's experience of maternity care 2010*

Chapter 5: Choosing to do childcare

1. Various evidence cited in: Fatherhood Institute (2010)
    Supporting Families and Relationships through Parental Leave

2. Cited in: Fatherhood Institute Research Summary (2011)
    Fathers, mothers, work and family

3. Deutsch, F. (2000) *Halving it All: How Equally Shared Parenting Works*,
    Harvard University Press

Chapter 6: Who's the daddy?

1. A mainstream parenting book that does tackle the father's role in
    parenting for the sake of the dad and child, not as some kind of
    assistant to the mother, is Brott, A. (2005) *The New Father: A Dad's
    Guide to the First Year*, Mitchell Beazley. A non-mainstream UK
    book which takes shared parenting as a key premise is Fisher, D.
    (2010) *Baby's Here: Who does what?* Grandma's Stories.

2. That's how to build a cabinet: David Cameron and Nick Clegg
    reveal they formed DIY coalition to build new cupboard for baby
    Florence, *Daily Mail*, 18 September 2010

3. Yates, C. (2012) *Fatherhood, UK political culture and the new politics*,
    Psychoanalysis, Culture & Society Vol. 17

4. Nick Clegg should run the country, not the kids to school,
    The Telegraph, 13 July 2011

5. Hen-pecked Cleggy should tell his wife that running the country
    matters more than doing the school run, *Daily Mail*, 13 July 2011

Chapter 7: Women vs men

1. Fatherhood Institute (2008) *The Difference a Dad Makes*

2. Lamb, M.E. [ed] (2010) *The Role of the Father in Child Development*,
    Wiley

3. Parke, R.D. (1981) *Fathering*, Fontana/Harvard University Press

4. Lamb, M.E. [ed] (2010)

5. White, Woollett & Lyon, *Fathers' involvement with their infants:
    the relevance of holding*, in: Fathers: Psychological Perspectives (1982)
    Junction.

6. Lewis, C. (1986) *Becoming a father*, Open University Press

7. Various evidence cited in: Fatherhood Institute (2010) *Supporting Families and Relationships through Parental Leave*

8. Parke, R.D. (1981)

9. National Childbirth Trust (2011) *Postnatal depression – the impact for women and children and interventions to enhance the mother-infant relationship*

10. Lamb, M.E. (1977) *Father-infant and mother-infant interaction in the first year of life*, in: Child Development, 48, Wiley

11. It's official - housework makes men happier, *Independent website*, 1 July 2012, http://www.independent.co.uk/voices/commentators/katy-guest-its-official--housework-makes-men-happier-7901744.html (accessed 12 December 2012)

12. Fathers are happier when doing more housework, *Guardian website*, 4 November 2010, http://www.guardian.co.uk/lifeandstyle/2010/nov/04/fathers-happier-more-housework-study (accessed 12 December 2012)

13. Office for National Statistics (2006) *Time Use, 2005 Edition*

14. Eight out of ten married women do more housework than their husbands, *IPPR website*, 10 Mar 2012, http://www.ippr.org/press-releases/111/8831/eight-out-of-ten-married-women-do-more-housework-than-their-husbands (accessed 13 December 2012)

15. Equal Opportunities Commission (2005) *Time Use and Childcare*

16. Cited in: Women will be doing the housework until 2050, *Telegraph website*, 20 May 2011, http://www.telegraph.co.uk/women/mother-tongue/8526413/Research-women-will-be-doing-the-housework-until-2050.html (accessed 13 December 2012)

17. Office for National Statistics (2006) *Time Use, 2005 Edition*, figure 4.4

18. Cited in: Fatherhood Institute (2011) *Family Man: British Fathers' Journey to the Centre of the Kitchen*

19. Cited in: Secret of a man's happiness: do the dishes for a quiet life, *Telegraph website*, 27 June 2012, http://www.telegraph.co.uk/women/mother-tongue/9356714/Secret-of-a-mans-happiness-do-the-dishes-for-a-quiet-life.html (accessed 13 December 2012)

20. Working Families (2011) *Working and Fathers: Combining family life and work*

Chapter 8: It's all work work work

1. Cited in: Fatherhood Institute (19 January 2011) *Fathers, mothers, work and family*

2. Demos (2011) *Reinventing the Workplace*

3. Fatherhood Institute (2011) *Family Man: British Fathers' Journey to the Centre of the Kitchen*

4. Fatherhood Institute (2011) *Family Man*

5. Number of women in cabinet falls, *Telegraph website, 4 September 2012,* http://www.telegraph.co.uk/news/politics/9520599/ Number-of-women-in-Cabinet-falls.html (accessed 4 January 2013)

Chapter 9: Doing the sums

1. The ONS recommends using men and women's hourly pay as the measure of the gender pay gap, because it strips out extra earnings from working longer hours, bonuses and other extras.

2. Office for National Statistics (November 2012) 2012 *Annual Survey of Hours and Earnings*, table 6.12a, tab: full-time

3. Gender pay gap 'at risk of worsening', say campaigners, *BBC News website,* http://www.bbc.co.uk/news/business-20223264 (accessed 12 December 2012)

4. Higher Education Statistics Agency (September 2012) *HE qualifications obtained by location of HE institution, mode of study, domicile, gender, level of qualification and class of first degree 2010/11,* Table 17

5. Cited in: Fatherhood Institute (19 January 2011) *Fathers, mothers, work and family*

6. On December 2012 tax regime allowances, if both parents earn £25k a year each, their total after-tax earnings would be £43,242. If one parent earned that £50k by themselves, the total after-tax would be £41,738 – about £1,500 less. If both parents earned £35k a year each, their total take-home would be £59,242, whereas if one parent earned that £70k alone it would be £53,738 – about £5,500 less. That's a very decent holiday's worth of difference, every single year. (National Insurance isn't included in these figures because it's even more complex, but it actually makes the difference even greater.)

Chapter 10: Flexible fatherhood

1. Office for National Statistics (2006) *Time Use, 2005 Edition*

2. Office for National Statistics (November 2012) *Statistical Bulletin: 2012 Annual Survey of Hours and Earnings*

3. Office for National Statistics (2008) *Focus on Gender*

4. TUC (2006) *Out of Time: Why Britain Needs a New Approach to Working-time Flexibility*

5. Cited in: Department for Business, Enterprise and Regulatory Reform (2008) *Right to request flexible working*

6. Equality and Human Rights Commission (2009) *Fathers, family and work: contemporary perspectives*

7. Department for Business, Innovation and Skills (2012) *Fourth Work Life Balance Employee Survey*, Table C4.2

8. Office for National Statistics (2008) *Focus on Gender*

9. Various information about flexible working rights at: Flexible working webguide, *Working Families website,* http://www.workingfamilies.org.uk/articles/parents-and-carers/flexible-working/flexible-working-webguide-step-1-what-to-ask-for (accessed 13 December 2012)

10. Various information about right to paid time off at: Time off for family and dependants, *Gov.uk website,* https://www.gov.uk/time-off-for-dependants/your-rights (accessed 13 December 2012)

11. Demos (2011) *Reinventing the Workplace*

12. Equality and Human Rights Commission (2009) *Meeting the changing needs of families, workers and employees in the 21st century*

13. Babies in the office: Who's been sleeping on my spreadsheet?, *Telegraph website,* 17 July 2012, http://www.telegraph.co.uk/women/mother-tongue/9403342/Babies-in-the-office-Whos-been-sleeping-on-my-spreadsheet.html (accessed 13 December 2012)

14. Bringing in baby, *The Guardian,* 8 April 2008

Chapter 11: Taking care

1. Grandparents Plus (2011) *Grandparents, childcare and employment: An analysis of British Social Attitudes Survey Data from 1998 and 2009*

2. Number of grandmothers: 1.4 million according to Grandparents Plus (2011); number of stay at home dads: 92,632 *(see Chapter 1, footnote 17)*; number of fathers who do the majority of childcare, according to Aviva: 784,000 *(see Chapter 1, footnotes 10 - 14)*.

3. Future Foundation (2012) *Division of responsibility in the home* (slide presentation)

Chapter 12: Making work work

1. Department for Education (2010) *Think Fathers: How flexible working for Dads can work for your business*

2. Equality and Human Rights Commission (2009) *Meeting the changing needs of families, workers and employees in the 21st century*

3. Drastic action, as well as statements of principle, needed to restore confidence, *Institute of Directors website, 9 May 2012, http://www. iod.com/Influencing/Press-Office/Press-releases/IoD-reaction-to-Queens-Speech-9-May-2012* (accessed 13 December 2012)

4. CBI comments: government consultation on parental leave and flexible working, *CBI website*, 16 May 2012,http://www.cbi. org.uk/media-centre/press-releases/2011/05/cbi-comments-government-consultation-on-parental-leave-and-flexible-working/ (accessed 13 December 2012)

5. Cited in: Fatherhood Institute (19 January 2011) *Fathers, mothers, work and family*

6. Working Families/Lancaster University Management School (2011) *Working and fathers: Combining family life and work*